EVERY DOLLAR MAKES A DIFFERENCE

the
better
world
SHOPPING
GUIDE

Ellis Jones

NEW SOCIETY PUBLISHERS

Cataloging in Publication Data:
A catalog record for this publication is available from the
National Library of Canada.

Cover concept by Ellis Jones. Design by Diane McIntosh.
Images: Getty Images/Photodisc Green.

Printed in Canada. Third printing November 2007.

Paperback ISBN-13: 978-0-86571-576-9
Paperback ISBN-10: 0-86571-576-9

Inquiries regarding requests to reprint all or part of
The Better World Shopping Guide should be addressed to
New Society Publishers at the address below.

To order directly from the publishers, please call toll-free
(North America) 1-800-567-6772, or order online at
www.newsociety.com

Any other inquiries can be directed by mail to:
New Society Publishers
P.O. Box 189, Gabriola Island, BC V0R 1X0, Canada
1-800-567-6772

New Society Publishers' mission is to publish books that
contribute in fundamental ways to building an ecologically
sustainable and just society, and to do so with the least possible impact on the environment, in a manner that models
this vision. We are committed to doing this not just through
education, but through action. We are acting on our commit-
ment to the world's remaining ancient forests by phasing
out our paper supply from ancient forests worldwide. This
book is one step toward ending global deforestation and
climate change. It is printed on acid-free paper that is **100%
old growth forest-free** (100% post-consumer recycled),
processed chlorine free, and printed with vegetable-based,
low-VOC inks. For further information, or to browse our full
list of books and purchase securely, visit our website at:
www.newsociety.com

NEW SOCIETY PUBLISHERS   www.newsociety.com

Contents

iv

APPRECIATION

I am very grateful to Paul Todisco and Ross Haenfler for their hard work testing the guide in the real world, and to my wonderful partner, Ara Francis, for her loving support during the long days and nights spent writing this book.

I am also very grateful to you, the reader, for picking up this book. I'd like to say (because you may never hear it from anyone else) on behalf of all of the people on this planet whom you will probably never meet and all the natural places you will probably never see...

Thank you.

BACKGROUND

After wrapping up *The Better World Handbook* in 2001 and a doctoral thesis on social responsibility a year later, I knew that my next major research project would be to create a comprehensive, up-to-date, reliable set of rankings on the social and environmental responsibility of businesses and corporations, and to make it available in a form that people could actually use in their everyday lives. You hold the result in your hands.

THE WEBSITE

This guide is far too small to contain the wide range of data that goes into generating the rankings for each company. If you're interested in more specifics on how individual companies are rated, and exactly what is taken into account, you can visit the website. It also contains updated rankings, direct links to resources, and new product categories that have been added since the writing of this guide. Take a look at the research behind the rankings online at:

www.betterworldshopper.org

THE PROBLEM

Money is power. Though you've probably heard this before, I'd like you to consider some of the special ramifications this has in our present society.

Wherever large amounts of money collect, so also new centers of power form. The latest historical manifestation of this is the modern corporation. As trillions of dollars accumulate in the corporate sphere, we witness the growing power of corporations to shape the world as they see fit.

This power is not limited to controlling the face of our own government through consistent record-breaking campaign contributions, but also the fate of millions of people and the planet itself through jobs, resource exploitation, pollution, working conditions, energy consumption, forest destruction, and so on.

These new power centers are not democracies. We don't vote for the CEO's or their policies (unless we are rich enough to be significant shareholders, who are informed enough to know what's going on, and compassionate enough to care about more than just personal profit), yet our destinies are increasingly in their hands.

THE SOLUTION

As these power centers shift, we must shift our own voices if we wish to be heard. As citizens, on average, we might vote once every four years, if at all. As consumers, we vote every single day with the purest form of power…money. The average American family spends around $18,000 every year on goods and services. Think of it as casting 18,000 votes every year for the kind of world you want to live in.

Unfortunately, as difficult as it is to find good, solid information on candidates during an election year, it's often even harder to find good, solid information on corporations. Our current laws are so lax, that half of the time we can't even figure out which brands belong to which companies (they don't have to tell us), much less have any idea of what their business practices look like.

For the past five years, I've dedicated myself to researching this very problem by compiling a database of every reliable source of information available on corporate behavior, and synthesized the information into a single report card grade for every company. The result is this book. Use it to reclaim your true vote. Use it to build a better world.

THE ISSUES

➤ **THE ENVIRONMENT:** rainforest destruction, pollution, recycling, renewable energy, eco-innovations, global warming, greenwashing, toxic waste dumping, sustainable farming.

➤ **HUMAN RIGHTS:** sweatshops, third-world community exploitation, international health issues, divestment, child labor.

➤ **COMMUNITY INVOLVEMENT:** volunteer efforts, local business support, sustainable growth, family farms.

➤ **ANIMAL PROTECTION:** humane treatment, factory farming, animal testing, animal habitat.

➤ **CORPORATE CRIME:** class action lawsuits, government fines, cover-ups, unethical business practices, illegal activities, political corruption, transparency.

➤ **DISCRIMINATION:** race, gender, age, ability, religion, sexuality, ethnicity, harassment.

➤ **EMPLOYEE TREATMENT:** health & safety records, union busting, fair wages, fatalities.

➤ **PHILANTHROPY:** donations, nonprofit alliances, establishing foundations.

THE SOURCES

Here is a short list of some of the resources used to assess the overall social responsibility of the companies included in this guide:

[BBB] Better Business Bureau: Torch Awards
[BE] Business Ethics: 100 Best Corporate Citizens
[CPI] Center for Public Integrity: Lobby Watch
[CAM] Co-op America: Green Business Certification
[CCC] Clean Computer Campaign
[CEP] Council on Economic Priorities
[CER] Covalence Ethical Rankings
[CK] Corporate Knights: 100 Most Sustainable Corporations
[CW] Corpwatch: Greenwash Awards
[EC] Ethical Consumer: Rankings & Boycotts List
[EPA] The U.S. Environmental Protection Agency
[FT] Transfair USA: Fair Trade Certification
[HRC] Human Rights Campaign: Equality Index
[MM] Multinational Monitor: 100 Worst Corporations
[PETA] People for Ethical Treatment of Animals
[TCP] The Ceres Principles: Sustainability Awards

THE 10 BEST LIST

1. SEVENTH GENERATION
2. PATAGONIA
3. AMERICAN APPAREL
4. EDEN FOODS
5. TOM'S OF MAINE
6. BEN & JERRY'S
7. WORKING ASSETS
8. CLIF BAR
9. STONYFIELD FARMS
10. AVEDA

The above list represents the 10 best companies on the planet based on their overall social and environmental records.

THE 10 WORST LIST

1. EXXON-MOBIL
2. ALTRIA (PHILIP MORRIS)
3. WAL-MART
4. CHEVRON-TEXACO
5. PFIZER
6. NESTLE
7. TYSON FOODS
8. GENERAL ELECTRIC
9. ARCHER DANIELS MIDLAND
10. GENERAL MOTORS

The above list represents the 10 worst companies on the planet based on their overall social and environmental records.

THE TOP 10 THINGS TO CHANGE

1. BANK
2. GASOLINE
3. SUPERMARKET
4. RETAIL STORES
5. CAR
6. SEAFOOD
7. CHOCOLATE
8. COFFEE
9. CREDIT CARD
10. CLEANING PRODUCTS

If you want to begin with the changes that will make the most difference for people and the planet, start with these ten things.

TEN SMALL BUT AMAZING BRANDS

1. DRUIDE
2. SHOREBANK
3. DR. BRONNER'S
4. MAGGIE'S ORGANICS
5. NEW BELGIUM BREWING
6. THANKSGIVING COFFEE
7. ENDANGERED SPECIES
8. EARTH TONES
9. HONEST TEA
10. TEN THOUSAND VILLAGES

The above list includes 10 small companies you may not have heard of that are true social and environmental leaders in their industries.

WHAT DO THE GRADES MEAN?

A	Often these companies were created specifically to provide socially and environmentally responsible options for consumers. A handful are merely responsibility leaders in their industry.
B	These companies tend to represent mainstream companies that are making significant progress in turning toward more people/planet friendly behaviors.
C	Companies that fall in the middle either have mixed responsibility records or insufficient data exists to rank them relative to the other companies.
D	If a company ends up here, it is involved in practices that have significantly negative consequences for humans and the environment.
F	This category is reserved for companies that are actively participating in the rapid destruction of the planet and the exploitation of human beings. Avoid these products at all costs.

WHAT IS ALL THIS EXTRA STUFF?

WHAT YOU NEED TO KNOW
This section will give you a thumbnail sketch of the current industry and its impact.

BUYING TIPS
Here you'll see tips that should help you maximize the positive impact of your dollar.

CORPORATE HERO
Company X

Examples of just a few of the things that put this particular company head and shoulders above the rest.

CORPORATE VILLAIN
Company Y

Examples of some of the things that land this company squarely at the bottom of the rankings.

RESOURCES
Here you'll find web links to sites that provide you with more information on the best companies or practices.

WHAT IF I CAN'T FIND A COMPANY?

While this guide is meant to be comprehensive, it is far from complete. You will likely encounter companies and brands on the shelves that don't show up in these pages. Here are a few simple guidelines that should help you:

If an unknown company's products are certified fair trade, you may assume that it falls into the A range.

If an unknown company's products are certified organic, you may assume that it falls into the A- or B+ range.

If you don't know anything at all about a particular company or brand, assume that it falls into the C range.

Unknown companies producing clothing and shoes should be assumed to have a D or F.

If you wish to see a more detailed version of these rankings or ask about a particular company that you can't find in the guide, you're welcome to visit: www.betterworldshopper.org

HOW TO USE THIS SHOPPING GUIDE

This book is meant to be used as a practical guide while shopping at the supermarket, in the mall, or online. Familiarize yourself with the alphabetical listing of categories and "dog-ear" any pages you find particularly useful.

Utilize the rankings on the left as a quick guide to any product you're thinking about buying. Note that all rankings are relative to their product category so that a company may shift up or down depending on its competition.

Useful information and helpful tips appear on the right along with a quick sketch of some of the differences between the best and worst companies. At the bottom of the page are links to online resources to learn more about some of the companies listed.

The book has been purposefully made small so that you can keep it with you in your purse, backpack, briefcase, or pocket. Find a convenient place for it now, while you're reading this sentence. Whatever you do, don't put it on a shelf!

AIRLINES

A	**A+**	
	A	
	A–	British Airways
B	**B+**	American Airlines
	B	Delta
	B–	Alaska Air, Horizon
C	**C+**	Singapore, Lufthansa, Japan Airlines, Air France
	C	
	C–	Korean Air
D	**D+**	Southwest, US Air
	D	United
	D–	Continental, Northwest
F	**F**	

AIRLINES

WHAT YOU NEED TO KNOW

Air travel has become so ubiquitous in our modern society that we often forget its significant environmental impact.

BUYING TIPS

✓ Green travel org's now offer carbon offsets to eliminate your flight's greenhouse gas impact

CORPORATE HERO

British Airways

☆ On CK's "100 Most Sustainable" list
☆ Industry leader in environment category
☆ Global climate change leadership award

CORPORATE VILLAIN

Northwest

☠ CEP "F" for overall social responsibility
☠ Refuses disclosure to consumers
☠ Racial profiling discrimination lawsuits

RESOURCES

⌨ www.sustainabletravelinternational.org
⌨ www.workingforchange.com/carbonfund

AUDIO EQUIPMENT

A	**A+**	
	A	
	A–	Apple, Sony
B	**B+**	
	B	
	B–	Panasonic, Philips, Sharp
C	**C+**	
	C	
	C–	JVC, Creative, RCA, Audiovox, GPX, Aiwa, Memorex, Koss, iRiver, Sennheiser, Labtec
D	**D+**	
	D	Samsung
	D–	Goldstar/LG
F	**F**	GE (General Electric)

AUDIO EQUIPMENT

WHAT YOU NEED TO KNOW
The wild success of portable audio players has transformed how we listen to music and news, but such items often end up leaching toxic chemicals in our landfills.

BUYING TIPS
✓ Choose electronics that are recyclable
✓ Look for products with Energy Star labels

CORPORATE HERO

Apple

☆ Perfect 100 on HRC Equality Index
☆ Free recycling take-back of iPods
☆ CEO limits own annual salary to $1

CORPORATE VILLAIN

GE (General Electric)

☠ MM's "Worst Corporation" list for 4 years
☠ #34 in "Top 100 Corporate Criminals"
☠ Target of "War Profiteer" campaign

RESOURCES
🖳 www.apple.com/environment

BABY CARE

A	**A+**	Seventh Generation
	A	Horizon
	A−	Healthy Times, Tushies, Organic Baby, Earth's Best, Tender Care
B	**B+**	Johnson & Johnson
	B	GoodNites, Huggies
	B−	Enfamil, Graco
C	**C+**	Gerber, Pampers, Luvs, Playtex
	C	
	C−	Del Monte
D	**D+**	Pedialyte, Pediasure, Similac
	D	
	D−	Nestle
F	**F**	Nabisco

BABY CARE

WHAT YOU NEED TO KNOW
Infants and toddlers are more vulnerable to the effects of harmful chemicals and pesticides, so if you're going to buy anything organic, it should be something from this category.

CORPORATE HERO
Seventh Generation

☆ Ranked #1 best company on the planet
☆ Empowers consumers w/packaging
☆ Winner, Sustainability Report Award
☆ Socially Responsible Business Award

CORPORATE VILLAIN
Nestle

☠ Baby formula human rights boycott
☠ "Most Irresponsible" corporation award
☠ Involved in child slavery lawsuit
☠ Aggressive takeovers of family farms

RESOURCES
🖳 www.seventhgen.com
🖳 www.healthytimes.com
🖳 www.earthsbest.com

BAKED GOODS & BAKING SUPPLIES

A	**A+**	Rapunzel, Eden
	A	King Arthur, Ener-G, Bob's Red Mill
	A–	Hain, Arrowhead Mills
B	**B+**	Betty Crocker, Pillsbury, Gold Medal
	B	Quaker, Fleischmann's
	B–	
C	**C+**	Scharffen Berger, Hershey's
	C	Rumford, Albers, Arm & Hammer, Ghirardelli, Krusteaz, Duncan Hines
	C–	Keebler, Borden
D	**D+**	Banquet, Diamond
	D	
	D–	Nestle, Carnation
F	**F**	Jell-O, Nabisco, Kraft

BAKED GOODS & BAKING SUPPLIES

BUYING TIPS
✓ Buy organic baking products when available

CORPORATE HERO

King Arthur Flour

☆ 100% employee-owned company
☆ Business Ethics award winner
☆ Partners with Stonyfield Farm (#9 best)
☆ BBB's Torch Award for ethics

CORPORATE VILLAIN

Kraft (Altria)

☠ MM's "Worst Corporation" list for 5 years
☠ Currently target of 2 major boycotts
☠ Greenwash Award for public deception
☠ Named global climate change laggard

RESOURCES
⌨ www.rapunzel.com
⌨ www.edenfoods.com
⌨ www.kingarthurflour.com
⌨ www.bobsredmill.com

BANKS & CREDIT CARDS

A	**A+**	
	A	ShoreBank, Chittenden, Wainwright, Alternatives Federal Credit Union, Working Assets
	A–	
B	**B+**	
	B	LOCAL CREDIT UNIONS
	B–	
C	**C+**	Bank One, Chase
	C	American Express
	C–	Bank Of America, Fleet, MBNA, Wells Fargo
D	**D+**	Wachovia, Capital One, Washington Mutual
	D	VISA, Compass Bank, Mastercard, First USA, US Bank, Discover
	D–	First Union
F	**F**	Diners Club, Citibank

For more detailed data visit – www.betterworldshopper.org

BANKS & CREDIT CARDS

WHAT YOU NEED TO KNOW

Where you put your money when you're not spending it is just as important as responsibly choosing what you spend it on. For your whole life (even while you sleep), that money will either be building a better world or tearing it down. While shopping, make your purchases doubly effective by using a credit card that donates a percentage of each purchase (over $5500/yr for the average American) to saving the planet.

BUYING TIPS

✓ Try using both a local bank AND an A bank
✓ Find out which credit unions are in your area
✓ Switch to a socially responsible credit card

RESOURCES

🖥 www.eco-bank.com
🖥 www.creditunion.coop/cu_locator
🖥 www.workingassets.com/creditcard

BEER

	A+	
A	A	New Belgium, Sierra Nevada
	A−	Wolaver's, Otter Creek, Eel River, Butte Creek
B	B+	Pete's, Full Sail, Alaskan, Rogue, Anchor
	B	Sam Adams
	B−	Amstel Light, Newcastle, Bass, Becks, Rolling Rock
C	C+	Molson, Killian's, Coors, Keystone, Zima
	C	Redhook, Michelob, Busch, King Cobra, Heineken, Budweiser
	C−	Tecate, Corona
D	D+	
	D	Guinness, Red Stripe
	D−	
F	F	Pabst Blue Ribbon, Miller, Milwaukee's Best, Henry Weinhard, Foster's

For more detailed data visit – www.betterworldshopper.org

BEER

BUYING TIPS

✓ Look for organic varieties of beer
✓ Buy from local microbreweries when possible
✓ Avoid buying beer in plastic bottles

CORPORATE HERO

New Belgium

☆ 1st 100% wind-powered brewery
☆ Conserves 50% more water vs. average
☆ Employee-owned business
☆ $1.6 million to local community

CORPORATE VILLAIN

Miller (Altria)

☠ Part of #2 worst company on the earth
☠ MM's "Worst Corporation" list for 5 years
☠ Currently target of 2 major boycotts
☠ Spent over $100 million on lobbyists

RESOURCES

🖳 www.newbelgium.com
🖳 www.sierranevada.com
🖳 www.wolavers.com
🖳 www.eelriverbrewing.com

BODY CARE

A	**A+**	Druide, Preserve
	A	Tom's of Maine, Aveda, Dr. Bronner's, Tweezerman
	A−	Burt's Bees, Kiss My Face, Jason, Aubrey, Aura Cacia
B	**B+**	Pure & Basic, Ecco Bella, Nature's Gate, EO
	B	Shikai, Avalon, Alba
	B−	Colgate, Speed Stick, Edge
C	**C+**	Gillette, Right Guard, Dry Idea, Soft & Dri
	C	Bic, Old Spice, Secret, Axe, Sure, Arrid, St. Ive's, Dove, Suave, Vaseline, Degree
	C−	Ban, Keri, Brut, Jergens, Blistex, Biore
D	**D+**	Mitchum, Banana Boat
	D	Schick, Coppertone
	D−	
F	**F**	Lubriderm, Chapstick

For more detailed data visit – www.betterworldshopper.org

BODY CARE

BUYING TIPS

✓ Avoid products tested on animals
✓ Seek out items made with organic ingredients
✓ Look for recyclable containers — #1, #2 plastic
✓ Buy larger quantities to reduce packaging

CORPORATE HERO

Tom's Of Maine

☆ Powered by 100% renewable energy
☆ Gives 10% of profits to nonprofits
☆ Part of #3 best company on the planet

CORPORATE VILLAIN

Lubriderm (Pfizer)

☠ #17 in "Top 100 Corporate Criminals"
☠ Worst environmental record in industry
☠ Continues unnecessary animal testing

RESOURCES

💻 www.tomsofmaine.com
💻 www.druide.ca
💻 www.recycline.com
💻 www.drbronner.com
💻 www.aveda.com

BREAD

A	**A +**	LOCAL BAKERY
	A	Alvarado Street
	A –	Rudi's Organic, Food For Life
B	**B +**	Pillsbury, Progresso
	B	
	B –	Weight Watchers, Sara Lee, Rainbo, Pepperidge Farm, Earth Grains
C	**C +**	Sun-Maid, Milton's
	C	Country Hearth, Boboli, Roman Meal, Tia Rosa, Thomas'
	C –	Oroweat
D	**D +**	
	D	Wonder, Home Pride, Colombo
	D –	
F	**F**	Kraft, Stove-Top

BREAD

WHAT YOU NEED TO KNOW
Despite all of our technological advancement, it's still a challenge to find a good, socially responsible loaf of bread in the supermarket.

BUYING TIPS
✓ Support a local bakery in your community

CORPORATE HERO

Alvarado Street

☆ Worker-owned cooperative
☆ PC socially responsible business award
☆ CAM certified Green Business

CORPORATE VILLAIN

Wonder (Interstate Bakeries)

☠ Major racial discrimination law suit
☠ Refuses disclosure to consumers
☠ CEP "F" for overall social responsibility

RESOURCES
🖥 www.alvaradostreetbakery.com
🖥 www.rudisbakery.com
🖥 www.food-for-life.com

BREAKFAST FOOD

A	**A+**	
	A	Amy's
	A−	Van's, Lifestream, Nature's Path, Envirokidz, Shelton's
B	**B+**	Pillsbury, General Mills, Betty Crocker
	B	Quaker
	B−	Hungry Jack, Morningstar Farms, Eggo, Kellogg's
C	**C+**	Hershey's, Weight Watchers, Jimmy Dean
	C	Kudos, Skippy, Golden Griddle, Entenmann's
	C−	
D	**D+**	
	D	Hormel
	D−	Armour, PAM
F	**F**	Nestle, Boca

BREAKFAST FOOD

WHAT YOU NEED TO KNOW
Every morning of your life, what you put on your plate for breakfast will determine what kind of world your children inherit in the future.

BUYING TIPS
✓ Buy at least one organic item for breakfast

CORPORATE HERO

Amy's Kitchen

☆ Donates food to relief efforts
☆ Produces all-vegetarian, organic foods
☆ CAM certified Green Business

CORPORATE VILLAIN

Hormel

☠ Supports inhumane factory farming
☠ Low score on HRC Equality Index
☠ Refuses disclosure to consumers

RESOURCES
🖥 www.amyskitchen.com
🖥 www.envirokidz.com
🖥 www.naturespath.com

BUTTER & MARGARINE

A	**A+**	Straus Family
	A	Horizon, Organic Valley, Spectrum
	A–	Organic Pastures
B	**B+**	Smart Balance, Earth Balance, Tillamook
	B	Benecol
	B–	Challenge
C	**C+**	
	C	
	C–	Land O' Lakes, Saffola, Canola Harvest
D	**D+**	I Can't Believe It's Not Butter, Country Crock, Imperial, Promise
	D	
	D–	
F	**F**	Blue Bonnet, Fleischmann's, Parkay

BUTTER & MARGARINE

BUYING TIPS
✓ Look for "No Hormones" and "No Antibiotics"
✓ Seek out items made with organic ingredients
✓ Avoid hydrogenated, saturated, and trans fats

CORPORATE HERO
Organic Valley
☆ Small family farmer-owned co-operative
☆ Gives 10% of profits to local community
☆ Humane animal treatment a priority

CORPORATE VILLAIN
Parkay (ConAgra)
☠ "Climate Change Laggard"
☠ MM's "Worst Corporation" list for 2 years
☠ #50 in "Top 100 Corporate Criminals"

RESOURCES
⌨ www.organicvalley.coop
⌨ www.strausmilk.com
⌨ www.horizonorganic.com

CANDY

A	A+	
	A	
	A–	Woodstock Farms, St. Claire's, Ginger People
B	B+	Haribo
	B	
	B–	Cadbury
C	C+	Jolly Ranchers, Good & Plenty, Hershey's, Andes, Heath, Twizzlers, Kit Kat, Almond Joy, Tootsie Roll, Mounds, Reese's
	C	Red Vines, Mike & Ike
	C–	LifeSavers
D	D+	Twix, Starburst, Skittles, M&Ms, Snickers, Milky Way, 3 Musketeers
	D	
	D–	
F	F	Kraft, Trolli, Nips, Wonka, Nestle, After Eight, Daim, Butterfinger

CANDY

WHAT YOU NEED TO KNOW

Most major candy manufacturers are also major chocolate purchasers, which currently means that they are using child slave labor to produce much of their candy. It's important to keep these companies accountable until they agree to basic human rights standards in the industry.

CORPORATE HERO

St. Claire's

☆ All products are certified organic
☆ 10% profits to rainforest medicine
☆ No animal by-products used (vegan)

CORPORATE VILLAIN

M&Ms (M&M/Mars)

☠ On MM's "10 Worst Corporations" list
☠ Suppliers use child slave labor
☠ Target of fair trade campaign

RESOURCES
⌨ www.globalexchange.org/cocoa
⌨ www.econaturalsolutions.com
⌨ www.gingerpeople.com

CANNED BEANS & CHILI

A	A+	Eden Foods
	A	Amy's
	A–	Walnut Acres, Westbrae, Bearitos
B	B+	Progresso
	B	
	B–	
C	C+	Campbell's
	C	Bush's, B&M, Nalley
	C–	Heinz
D	D+	S&W, Stagg, Hormel, Dinty Moore
	D	
	D–	Dennison's, Rosarita, Van Camp's
F	F	Libby's, Ortega, Taco Bell

CANNED BEANS & CHILI

WHAT YOU NEED TO KNOW
Some of the most socially responsible companies now provide a wide variety of canned goods that should be available at most supermarkets.

CORPORATE HERO

Eden Foods

☆ Ranked #9 best company on the planet
☆ CEP's highest social responsibility score
☆ CAM certified Green Business

CORPORATE VILLAIN

Hormel

☣ Supports inhumane factory farming
☣ Low score on HRC Equality Index
☣ Refuses disclosure to consumers

RESOURCES
🖥 www.edenfoods.com
🖥 www.amyskitchen.com
🖥 www.westbrae.com
🖥 www.walnutacres.com

CANNED FRUIT & VEGETABLES

A	**A+**	
	A	Muir Glen, Santa Cruz Organic
	A–	Westbrae
B	**B+**	Progresso, Green Giant
	B	
	B–	Dole
C	**C+**	Mott's
	C	Sunsweet, Tree Top, Oregon, Glory Foods, Ocean Spray
	C–	French's
D	**D+**	Del Monte, S&W, Contadina
	D	
	D–	
F	**F**	Libby's

CANNED FRUIT & VEGETABLES

WHAT YOU NEED TO KNOW

While "organic" has become increasingly popular in fresh produce sections of supermarkets, there is a small, but growing, selection of canned fruits and vegetables available on the aisle shelves.

CORPORATE HERO

Muir Glen

☆ First organic tomato processor in US
☆ CAM certified Green Business
☆ Environmental leader in food industry

CORPORATE VILLAIN

Libby's (Altria)

☠ Greenwash Award for public deception
☠ Named global climate change laggard
☠ Undermines overseas health standards

RESOURCES

🖥 www.muirglen.com
🖥 www.westbrae.com
🖥 www.scojuice.com

CARS

A	**A+**	
	A	
	A –	Toyota, Lexus, Scion
B	**B+**	Honda, Acura
	B	
	B –	Volkswagen, Subaru
C	**C +**	Porsche, Mazda
	C	Audi, Suzuki
	C –	Hyundai, Kia, BMW
D	**D+**	Isuzu, Ford, Jaguar, Volvo, Land Rover, Lincoln, Mercury, Mini
	D	Infiniti, Nissan, Jeep, Dodge, Chrysler, Mercedes
	D –	Mitsubishi
F	**F**	Buick, Cadillac, Saturn, Chevrolet, GMC, Saab, Hummer, Pontiac

CARS

BUYING TIPS:
- ✓ Look for cars that get at least 30 MPG
- ✓ Think about a hybrid vehicle for your next car
- ✓ Consider buying carbon offsets for your car

CORPORATE HERO

Toyota

- ☆ Ranked #1 most ethical automaker
- ☆ Industry leader in fighting climate change
- ☆ EPA Green Power Leader award winner
- ☆ Created an $8 billion diversity program

CORPORATE VILLAIN

General Motors

- ☠ Named #1 polluter in auto industry
- ☠ Leader in fighting clean air legislation
- ☠ EPA designated plant as Superfund site
- ☠ Paid $50 million to Washington lobbyists

RESOURCES

- 🖥 www.fueleconomy.gov
- 🖥 www.betterworldclub.com
- 🖥 www.terrapass.com
- 🖥 www.prius.com

CEREAL

A	**A+**	
	A	Cascadian Farm
	A–	Health Valley, Arrowhead Mills, Peace Cereal, Nature's Path, Envirokidz, Barbara's
B	**B+**	General Mills, Pillsbury
	B	Quaker, Mother's
	B–	
C	**C+**	Kelloggs, Kashi
	C	
	C–	
D	**D+**	Weight Watchers
	D	
	D–	
F	**F**	Post, Kraft, Nabisco

CEREAL

WHAT YOU NEED TO KNOW
Currently, choosing a socially responsible cereal is one of the easiest ways to make a difference with your dollars. There are a wide variety of excellent choices available in most supermarkets.

CORPORATE HERO
Peace Cereal

☆ 10% profits to peace building
☆ Sponsors socially responsible awards
☆ Offers complete line of organic cereals

CORPORATE VILLAIN
Post (Altria)

☠ Part of #2 worst company on the earth
☠ MM's "Worst Corporation" list for 5 years
☠ Currently target of 2 major boycotts
☠ Named global climate change laggard

RESOURCES
🖳 www.cascadianfarm.com
🖳 www.peacecereal.com
🖳 www.barbarasbakery.com
🖳 www.envirokidz.com

CHIPS

A	A+	Kettle Chips
	A	
	A-	Garden of Eatin', Terra Chips, Little Bear, Bearitos
B	B+	Bugles, Snyder's
	B	Cheetos, Lay's, Doritos, Fritos, Tostitos, Sun Chips, Funyuns, Ruffles
	B-	Pringles
C	C+	Pepperidge Farm
	C	Mission, Cape Cod, Guiltless Gourmet, Robert's, Eat Smart, Genisoy, Boulder
	C-	
D	D+	French's
	D	
	D-	
F	F	Nabisco

CHIPS

BUYING TIPS

✓ Look for chips made with organic ingredients
✓ Avoid hydrogenated, saturated, and trans fats
✓ Buy larger quantities to reduce packaging

CORPORATE HERO

Kettle Chips

☆ 100% of waste oil turned into biodiesel
☆ Restored local wetlands habitat
☆ One of the largest solar arrays in NW
☆ Gives tons of potatoes to hunger orgs

CORPORATE VILLAIN

Nabisco (Altria)

☠ Greenwash Award for public deception
☠ Continues to do business in Burma
☠ Named global climate change laggard
☠ Refuses to disclose data on diversity
☠ Spent over $100 million on lobbyists

RESOURCES

🖥 www.kettlefoods.com
🖥 www.terrachips.com
🖥 www.gardenofeatin.com

CHOCOLATE

A	A+	Endangered Species, Equal Exchange, Rapunzel, Dagoba
	A	Green & Black's
	A−	Newman's Own, Cloud Nine, Tropical Source, Shaman
B	B+	
	B	
	B−	Cadbury
C	C+	Hershey's, Scharffen Berger
	C	Ferrero Rocher, Russell Stover, Chocolove, Whitman's, Ghirardelli, Lindt, Droste
	C−	
D	D+	Dove
	D	
	D−	Swiss Miss
F	F	Nestle, Perugina, Toblerone

CHOCOLATE

WHAT YOU NEED TO KNOW
Recently, the ILO, UNICEF and US State Department uncovered the widespread use of child slave labor in the chocolate industry — up to 40% of all chocolate is currently being produced in this way.

BUYING TIPS
✓ Companies in the A category are slave-free
✓ Look for chocolate that is fair trade certified
✓ Buy organic chocolate when available

CORPORATE HERO

Endangered Species

☆ Fair trade, organic, slave-free chocolate
☆ Suppliers = small, family-owned farms
☆ Eco-certified (LEED) production plant
☆ 10% of profits donated to wildlife groups

CORPORATE VILLAIN

Nestle

☠ "Most Irresponsible" corporation award
☠ Aggressive takeovers of family farms
☠ Involved in child slavery lawsuit
☠ Baby formula human rights boycott

CIGARETTES

A	**A+**	
	A	
	A−	American Spirit
B	**B+**	
	B	
	B−	Nat Sherman
C	**C+**	
	C	
	C−	
D	**D+**	GPC, Lucky Strike, Viceroy, Camel, Kool, Winston, Capri, Salem, Carlton
	D	Dunhill
	D−	
F	**F**	Marlboro, Pall Mall, Virginia Slims, Basic, Benson & Hedges, Chesterfield, L&M, Parliament, West, Merit

CIGARETTES

WHAT YOU NEED TO KNOW

"Big Tobacco" has been successfully prosecuted in the US for everything from marketing campaigns aimed at kids to covering up the addictive nature and dangerous side-effects of smoking, but the negative impacts of their original actions will be felt for generations to come. Also, some of these practices continue unabated in countries outside the US.

CORPORATE HERO

American Spirit

☆ Only producer of organic cigarettes
☆ Does not test its products on animals
☆ Uses 100% additive-free tobacco
☆ Donates to American Indian causes

CORPORATE VILLAIN

Marlboro (Altria)

☠ Named "Top 10 Greenwasher"
☠ Involved in document deletion cover-up
☠ Undermines overseas health standards
☠ #1 contributor to Washington lobbyists
☠ MM's "Worst Corporation" list for 5 years

CLEANING PRODUCTS

A	**A+**	Seventh Generation
	A	Ecover, Dr. Bronner's
	A–	Orange-Mate, Citra-Solv, Planet, ECOS, Lifetree, Earth Friendly
B	**B+**	
	B	Simple Green
	B–	SC Johnson, Drano, Dial, Fantastik, Windex, Ziploc
C	**C+**	Colgate Palmolive, Murphy's Oil, 3M
	C	Dawn, Procter & Gamble
	C–	
D	**D+**	Hefty, Quickie, WD-40, Arm & Hammer
	D	Chore Boy, Sara Lee, Wizard, Reckitt Benckiser
	D–	
F	**F**	Pine Sol, Tilex, Clorox, S.O.S., Glad, Liquid-Plumr

For more detailed data visit – www.betterworldshopper.org

CLEANING PRODUCTS

BUYING TIPS
✓ Look for non-petroleum based products
✓ Avoid products with chlorine/toxic chemicals

CORPORATE HERO

Seventh Generation

☆ #1 best company on the planet
☆ Empowers consumers w/packaging
☆ Winner, Sustainability Report Award
☆ Socially Responsible Business Award

CORPORATE VILLAIN

Clorox

☠ On MM's "10 Worst Corporations" list
☠ Continues unnecessary animal testing
☠ Refuses disclosure to consumers
☠ Major producer of chlorine — dioxin

RESOURCES
🖥 www.seventhgeneration.com
🖥 www.ecover.com
🖥 www.drbronner.com

CLOTHING

A	**A+**	Patagonia, American Apparel
	A	Maggies Organics, Ecolution
	A−	Deva Lifewear
B	**B+**	Levi Strauss, Timberland, Liz Claiborne, Cutter & Buck
	B	LL Bean, Nordstrom, Nike
	B−	Van Heusen, Bass, DKNY, FUBU, Nicole Miller
C	**C+**	Target, Gap, Mervyn's
	C	
	C−	JC Penney, Macy's, Foley's, Marshall Fields, Lord & Taylor
D	**D+**	Fruit of the Loom, Land's End, Limited, Jones Apparel, Kmart, Perry Ellis, Guess
	D	Ralph Lauren, Polo, Calvin Klein, Bill Blass, LA Gear
	D−	Vanity Fair, TJ Maxx, Kohl's, Marshall's, Consolidated
F	**F**	Wal-Mart, Sam's Club, Dillard's

For more detailed data visit – www.betterworldshopper.org

CLOTHING

WHAT YOU NEED TO KNOW
The fact is that many of the clothes we wear today are made in sweatshops in the developing world. Better companies have either US made clothing or strictly enforced human rights standards that ensure fair wages and safe working conditions.

CORPORATE HERO
American Apparel

☆ Makes organic, sweatshop-free clothes
☆ Highest standard in the industry
☆ Workers make $15/hr vs. $.09/hr

CORPORATE VILLAIN
Dillard's

☠ No code of conduct for sweatshops
☠ Refuses disclosure on its business
☠ Named "Sweatshop Laggard" by CEP

RESOURCES
🖥 www.cleanclothes.org
🖥 www.americanapparel.net
🖥 www.patagonia.com

COFFEE

A	**A+**	Thanksgiving, Song Bird
	A	Equal Exchange, Café Mam, Caffe Ibis, Green Mountain, Adam's, Newman's Own Organic
	A–	LOCAL COFFEE SHOPS
B	**B+**	
	B	Starbucks
	B–	Peerless, Peet's, Seattle's Best
C	**C+**	Millstone, Folgers
	C	Continental, Hill Bros, MJB
	C–	
D	**D+**	
	D	International Delight
	D–	Nescafe, Nestle
F	**F**	Maxwell House, Gevalia, Sanka, General Foods, Yuban

COFFEE

WHAT YOU NEED TO KNOW
Global coffee prices have plummeted recently, pushing some coffee farmers in the developing world to the brink of starvation. Buying fair trade coffee is now more important than ever.

BUYING TIPS
✓ Look for fair trade, shade grown, organic
✓ Support local, independent coffee shops

CORPORATE HERO

Thanksgiving Coffee

☆ Supports religious tolerance & wildlife
☆ Uses biodiesel trucks for transportation

CORPORATE VILLAIN

Nescafe (Nestle)

☠ Involved in union busting outside US
☠ "Bottom Rung", Ladder of Responsibility

RESOURCES
🖥 www.transfairusa.org
🖥 www.thanksgivingcoffee.com
🖥 www.equalexchange.com

COMPUTERS & ACCESSORIES

A	**A+**	
	A	
	A–	HP, Compaq, IBM, Intel
B	**B+**	Sony, Apple, Motorola
	B	Fujitsu, Toshiba, Canon, Lexmark, Dell
	B–	NEC, Packard Bell, Hitachi, Epson
C	**C+**	AMD, Brother, NCR, Panasonic, Oki
	C	Sanyo, Sharp, Philips, JVC
	C–	Micron, Viewsonic
D	**D+**	eMachines
	D	Samsung, Goldstar/LG, Gateway
	D–	Acer, AST
F	**F**	Mitsubishi

COMPUTERS & ACCESSORIES

WHAT YOU NEED TO KNOW

Computers have become an essential part of everyday life for many of us, but that need to stay up-to-date has also led to a rapidly growing problem of toxic computer waste in our landfills.

CORPORATE HERO

HP (Hewlett Packard)

☆ Free return recycling of its computers
☆ Perfect 100 on HRC Equality Index
☆ Countless awards for business ethics

CORPORATE VILLAIN

Acer

☠ Well-documented use of sweatshops
☠ CCC Failing grade for environment
☠ Serious customer privacy violations

RESOURCES

⌨ www.svtc.org/cleancc
⌨ www.computertakeback.com
⌨ www.hp.com

CONDIMENTS

A	**A+**	Eden
	A	Annie's, Spectrum, Muir Glen, Hain, Hollywood, Westbrae, Vegenaise
	A–	Woodstock Farms
B	**B+**	Natural Value
	B	
	B–	Bragg's
C	**C+**	
	C	San-J, Saffola, Lea & Perrins, McCormick, Tabasco, Kikkoman, Mrs. Dash
	C–	Best Foods, Lawry's, French's
D	**D+**	Heinz, Del Monte
	D	KC Masterpiece
	D–	La Choy, Gulden's
F	**F**	Miracle Whip, Kraft, Bull's Eye, A1, Grey Poupon

CONDIMENTS

WHAT YOU NEED TO KNOW

Whether you're looking for ketchup, mustard, mayonnaise, barbeque sauce, or soy sauce, there are now socially responsible brands of each.

BUYING TIPS

✓ Choose organic condiments when available

CORPORATE HERO

Spectrum

☆ Uses eco-certification for int'l suppliers
☆ Partners with int'l worker co-ops
☆ Promotes small-scale, sustainable farms

CORPORATE VILLAIN

Kraft (Altria)

☠ Named "Top 10 Greenwasher"
☠ Involved in document deletion cover-up
☠ Continues to do business in Burma

RESOURCES

🖳 www.spectrumorganics.com
🖳 www.edenfoods.com

COOKIES

A	**A+**	
	A	Barbara's
	A –	Alternative Baking Co., Sun Flour Baking Co., Nature's Choice, Health Valley, Country Choice Organic, Nature's Path, Immaculate, Newman's Own Organic, Organica
B	**B +**	Mi-del
	B	Mother's
	B –	Keebler
C	**C +**	Pepperidge Farm
	C	Pamela's, LU, Archway
	C –	
D	**D +**	Dove
	D	
	D –	
F	**F**	Nabisco

COOKIES

WHAT YOU NEED TO KNOW
The socially responsible cookie industry has recently exploded, so there's no longer any need to feel guilty about reaching into the cookie jar.

CORPORATE HERO

Newman's Own

☆ 100% of profits to education & charity
☆ CEP "A" for overall social responsibility
☆ Given over $200 million to good causes

CORPORATE VILLAIN

Nabisco (Altria)

☠ Part of #2 worst company on the earth
☠ Currently the target of 2 major boycotts
☠ Spent over $100 million on lobbyists
☠ Greenwash Award for public deception

RESOURCES
🖥 www.newmansownorganics.com
🖥 www.barbarasbakery.com
🖥 www.organicafoods.com
🖥 www.countrychoicenaturals.com
🖥 www.healthvalley.com

COSMETICS

A	**A+**	
	A	Aveda
	A−	Burt's Bees, Aubrey Organics, Kiss My Face, Zia, The Body Shop
B	**B+**	Ecco Bella, EO, Dr. Hauschka
	B	Avalon Organics, Zuzu, Triloka, Gabriel, Desert Essence
	B−	Aveeno, Neutrogena, Johnson & Johnson
C	**C+**	Max Factor, Olay, Covergirl
	C	Chesebrough Ponds, Pond's, Dove
	C−	Nivea, Cutex
D	**D+**	La Cross, Sally Hansen
	D	Maybelline, L'Oreal
	D−	
F	**F**	Almay, Revlon

COSMETICS

WHAT YOU NEED TO KNOW
While some cosmetics companies still carry out tests on animals, many smaller companies now provide animal and eco-friendly alternatives.

BUYING TIPS
✓ Choose companies that don't test on animals
✓ Look for products with organic ingredients

CORPORATE HERO

Aveda

☆ Products never tested on animals
☆ Perfect score for social responsibility
☆ Sustainable sourcing of ingredients

CORPORATE VILLAIN

Maybelline (L'Oreal)

☠ Continues unnecessary animal testing
☠ Ingredients include known carcinogens
☠ Company a target of 2 major boycotts

RESOURCES
💻 www.aveda.com
💻 www.caringconsumer.com

CRACKERS

A	**A+**	
	A	Annie's, Barbara's
	A−	Health Valley, Hain
B	**B+**	Sesmark, Edward & Sons
	B	Masuya, Ryvita
	B−	Keebler, Sunshine, Carr's, Kashi
C	**C+**	Pepperidge Farm
	C	
	C−	
D	**D+**	Ry Krisp, Wasa, Old London, Lance
	D	
	D−	
F	**F**	Kraft, Nabisco

CRACKERS

WHAT YOU NEED TO KNOW
Once rare in the US, organic wheat is now a popular choice for many small, family farmers.

BUYING TIPS
✓ Purchase organic crackers when available

CORPORATE HERO

Annie's

☆ Regularly donates products to nonprofits
☆ Created environmental studies scholarship
☆ Supports organic, family farms

CORPORATE VILLAIN

Nabisco (Altria)

☠ MM's "Worst Corporation" list for 5 years
☠ Greenwash Award for public deception
☠ Spent over $100 million on lobbyists
☠ Involved in document deletion cover-up

RESOURCES
💻 www.annies.com
💻 www.barbarasbakery.com
💻 www.healthvalley.com

DAIRY ALTERNATIVES

A	**A+**	Silk
	A	Follow Your Heart, Stonyfield Farms, Nancy's, Wildwood
	A–	WholeSoy, ZenSoy
B	**B+**	Tofu/Vegan/Almond Rella, Soya Kaas
	B	
	B–	
C	**C+**	
	C	Lisanatti, Tofutti, Soy Moon, Soyco, Galaxy Nutritional, Soymage, Veggie/Rice Slice
	C–	Borden
D	**D+**	
	D	International Delight
	D–	Carnation
F	**F**	Cool Whip

DAIRY ALTERNATIVES

BUYING TIPS
✓ Choose organic products when available
✓ Look for items with easily recycled
  containers

CORPORATE HERO

Silk (White Wave)

☆ Actively supports small, family farms
☆ Powered by 100% renewable energy
☆ Industry environmental leader
☆ EPA "Green Partner Of The Year"

CORPORATE VILLAIN

Cool Whip (Altria)

☠ Named global climate change laggard
☠ Undermines overseas health standards
☠ #1 contributor to Washington lobbyists
☠ Continues to do business in Burma

RESOURCES
🖥 www.silksoymilk.com
🖥 www.stonyfield.com
🖥 www.nancysyogurt.com

DAIRY PRODUCTS

A	**A+**	Straus Family
	A	Horizon, Stonyfield Farms, Brown Cow
	A –	Organic Valley, Helios, Tillamook
B	**B+**	Lifeway, Cabot, Organic Creamery, Greenbank Farms, Alta Dena
	B	Yoplait
	B –	Lactaid
C	**C+**	
	C	Sargento, Precious, Pavel's, Mountain High, Dannon, Kozy Shack, Cascade Fresh, Crystal
	C –	Continental
D	**D+**	
	D	Hunt's, Reddi-Wip
	D –	Nestle
F	**F**	Knudsen, Jell-O, Kraft

DAIRY PRODUCTS

WHAT YOU NEED TO KNOW

While large corporate farms are the norm for the dairy industry, many small, family farms are fighting back by going organic in order to survive.

BUYING TIPS

✓ Look for "No Hormones" and "No Antibiotics"
✓ Choose items made with organic ingredients

CORPORATE HERO

Stonyfield Farms

☆ 10% of profits to environmental groups
☆ Received Business Ethics Award
☆ Winner of numerous eco-awards

CORPORATE VILLAIN

Kraft (Altria)

☠ Part of #2 worst company on the earth
☠ Currently the target of 2 major boycotts
☠ Greenwash Award for public deception

RESOURCES

💻 www.stonyfield.com
💻 www.horizonorganic.com

DENTAL CARE

A	**A+**	Preserve
	A	Tom's of Maine
	A–	Jason, Burt's Bees, Kiss My Face, Ecodent
B	**B+**	Radius, Nature's Gate, Auromere, Natural Dentist, Desert Essence
	B	ACT, Reach, Rembrandt, Johnson & Johnson
	B–	Colgate
C	**C+**	Scope, Oral-B, Crest
	C	POH, GUM, Mentadent, Arm & Hammer, Fuchs
	C–	
D	**D+**	
	D	Aquafresh, Sensodyne
	D–	
F	**F**	Listerine

DENTAL CARE

WHAT YOU NEED TO KNOW
Smaller, environmentally friendly companies now offer increasingly popular alternatives to the dental products of larger, mainstream corporations.

BUYING TIPS
- ✓ Look for products made with recycled content
- ✓ Buy items with easily recycled packaging

CORPORATE HERO
Preserve (Recycline)

- ☆ Environmental leader in industry
- ☆ Products from 100% recycled plastic
- ☆ Take-back recycling of all products

CORPORATE VILLAIN
Listerine (Pfizer)

- ☠ Worst environmental record in industry
- ☠ MM's "Worst Corporation" list for 4 years
- ☠ Paid $44 million to Washington lobbyists

RESOURCES
- 💻 www.recycline.com
- 💻 www.tomsofmaine.com

DESSERTS

A	**A+**	
	A	Amy's, Ah!Laska
	A–	
B	**B+**	Wholly Wholesome
	B	
	B–	Sara Lee, Weight Watchers
C	**C+**	Pepperidge Farm
	C	Mrs. Smith's, Claim Jumper
	C–	
D	**D+**	
	D	Marie Callender's, Reddi-wip
	D–	
F	**F**	Kraft, Cool Whip, Jell-O

DESSERTS

WHAT YOU NEED TO KNOW
If you don't have time to bake your own pie
from the apple tree in your back yard, your best
option is to buy an organic apple pie from the
store.

BUYING TIPS
✓ Look for items made with organic ingredients

CORPORATE HERO
Amy's Kitchen
☆ Donates food to relief efforts
☆ Produces all-vegetarian, organic foods
☆ CAM certified Green Business

CORPORATE VILLAIN
Jell-O (Altria)
☻ Named "Top 10 Greenwasher"
☻ Involved in document deletion cover-up
☻ Continues to do business in Burma
☻ Currently the target of 2 major boycotts

RESOURCES
🖥 www.amyskitchen.com
🖥 www.whollywholesome.com

EGGS

A	**A+**	
	A	Horizon Organic, Organic Valley
	A−	Humane Harvest, Veg-a-Fed, Mother's, Chino Valley, Clover Stornetta, Judy's Family Farm
B	**B+**	
	B	
	B−	Eggology
C	**C+**	Rock Island
	C	Gold Circle Farms, Egglands Best
	C−	Nulaid
D	**D+**	Lucerne
	D	
	D−	
F	**F**	Egg Beaters

EGGS

WHAT YOU NEED TO KNOW
Factory farming has made egg production today a cruel and environmentally damaging endeavor. Seek out smaller, more humane options.

BUYING TIPS
✓ Look for cage-free or free-range eggs
✓ Buy organic eggs whenever possible
✓ Seek out recycled paper-based packaging

CORPORATE HERO
Organic Valley

☆ Small, family farmer-owned cooperative
☆ Gives 10% of profits to local community
☆ Humane animal treatment a priority

CORPORATE VILLAIN
EggBeaters (ConAgra)

☠ Involved in major accounting scandal
☠ 2nd largest E. coli meat recall in history
☠ Many worker safety & health violations

RESOURCES
⌨ www.horizonorganic.com

ELECTRONICS

A	**A+**	
	A	
	A–	Apple, Sony, Aiwa, Kodak
B	**B+**	
	B	Toshiba
	B–	Duracell, Hitachi, Sharp, Philips, Panasonic
C	**C+**	Fuji
	C	Sanyo, TDK, Pioneer, Haier, Apex, JVC, RCA, Koss, Magnavox, Kenwood, Nintendo
	C–	Microsoft
D	**D+**	Samsung, Goldstar/LG
	D	Energizer, Daewoo
	D–	Mitsubishi
F	**F**	GE (General Electric)

ELECTRONICS

WHAT YOU NEED TO KNOW

Our addiction to the latest electronics has
created a significant drain on our energy grid
(even when they're off!) as well as a major
recycling problem.

BUYING TIPS

✓ Look for electronics with Energy Star labels
✓ Buy rechargeable (NiMH) batteries
✓ Choose electronics that are recyclable

CORPORATE HERO

Sony

☆ Environmental leader in industry
☆ Sustainable business award winner
☆ CER #2 "Best Ethical Ranking"

CORPORATE VILLAIN

GE (General Electric)

☠ Major weapons producer including land-
  mines
☠ Creator of 5 Superfund sites
☠ Target of environmental boycott

RESOURCES

🖥 www.sony.net/SonyInfo/Environment

ENERGY BARS

A	**A+**	
	A	CLIF, Luna, Alpsnack
	A−	BumbleBar, Larabar
B	**B+**	Health Valley
	B	Think, Nutiva, Boomi
	B−	Nature Valley, Quaker
C	**C+**	Kashi, Odwalla
	C	
	C−	Slim Fast, Kudos
D	**D+**	
	D	
	D−	Powerbar
F	**F**	Balance

ENERGY BARS

WHAT YOU NEED TO KNOW
Because many energy bar companies have truly stepped up to the plate, your choice of energy bar is one of the easiest ways to make a powerful difference for people and the planet.

CORPORATE HERO
CLIF

☆ #7 best company on the earth
☆ Winner, Business Ethics Award
☆ EPA Green Power Leader award winner

CORPORATE VILLAIN
Balance (Altria)

☠ Part of #2 worst company on the earth
☠ Named global climate change laggard
☠ Undermines overseas health standards
☠ #1 contributor to Washington lobbyists

RESOURCES
💻 www.clifbar.com
💻 www.alpsnack.com
💻 www.bumblebar.com
💻 www.larabar.com

ENERGY DRINKS

A	**A+**	
	A	Bossa Nova
	A–	
B	**B+**	Monster, Energy
	B	Gatorade, SoBe, Starbucks, AMP, Propel
	B–	Lipton
C	**C+**	Snapple
	C	Fuze, Red Bull, Bawls, Glaceau, Arizona, Rockstar
	C–	
D	**D+**	
	D	Full Throttle, Powerade
	D–	
F	**F**	Tang, Kool-Aid, Country Time, Crystal Light

ENERGY DRINKS

WHAT YOU NEED TO KNOW
While there are few "great" socially responsible choices for energy drinks, its important to choose good options, which are readily available.

BUYING TIPS
✓ Buy drinks in aluminum or glass containers

CORPORATE HERO
Bossa Nova

☆ Plants a tree for every bottle purchased
☆ Uses wild harvested, rainforest plants
☆ Works directly with Rainforest Alliance

CORPORATE VILLAIN
Full Throttle (Coke)

☠ MM's "Worst Corporation" list for 3 years
☠ Hinders clean water access abroad
☠ Target of major human rights boycotts

RESOURCES
🖥 www.bossausa.com
🖥 www.stopcorporateabuse.org
🖥 www.cokewatch.org

FEMININE CARE

A	**A+**	Gladrags
	A	Seventh Generation
	A–	Organic Essentials, Natracare
B	**B+**	
	B	Stayfree, Carefree, O.B.
	B–	
C	**C+**	Kotex, Poise
	C	
	C–	Always, Tampax
D	**D+**	
	D	GENERIC BRANDS
	D–	
F	**F**	

FEMININE CARE

WHAT YOU NEED TO KNOW
Much of the effort for socially responsible business has been driven by women, so it's not surprising that there are many great options in this category.

BUYING TIPS
✓ Buy care products with less packaging waste

CORPORATE HERO

Seventh Generation

☆ Ranked #1 best company on the planet
☆ Empowers consumers w/packaging
☆ Socially Responsible Business Award

CORPORATE VILLAIN

Tampax (P&G)

☠ MM's "Worst Corporation" list for 2 years
☠ Continues unnecessary animal testing
☠ Target of major consumer boycott

RESOURCES
🖥 www.gladrags.com
🖥 www.natracare.com
🖥 www.seventhgen.com

FROZEN DINNERS

A	**A+**	
	A	Amy's, Ethnic Gourmet
	A −	Rising Moon, Organic Classics, Moosewood, Cedarlane, Seeds of Change
B	**B+**	
	B	Totino's
	B −	
C	**C+**	Weight Watchers
	C	Swanson, Hungry Man, Foster Farms, Quorn, Michelina's, Red Baron
	C −	Bertolli, Birds Eye
D	**D+**	Uncle Ben's, Boston Market, TGI Friday's
	D	
	D −	Healthy Choice, Marie Callendar's, Banquet
F	**F**	Boca, Stouffer's, Hot Pockets

FROZEN DINNERS

WHAT YOU NEED TO KNOW
Today's stress-filled lifestyles have created increasing demand for quick and easy meals. Luckily, a number of responsible companies have decided to focus on options that are good for people and the planet.

CORPORATE HERO

Amy's Kitchen

☆ Donates food to relief efforts
☆ Produces all-vegetarian, organic foods
☆ CAM certified Green Business

CORPORATE VILLAIN

Stouffer's (Nestle)

☗ Aggressive takeovers of family farms
☗ Baby formula human rights boycott
☗ "Most Irresponsible" corporation award
☗ Involved in union busting outside US

RESOURCES
⌨ www.amyskitchen.com
⌨ www.fairfieldfarmkitchens.com
⌨ www.risingmoon.com

FRUIT & VEGETABLES

A	**A+**	FARMERS MARKETS, CSAs
	A	Earthbound Farm, Cascadian Farm
	A–	Newman's Own, Sno Pac, Sunridge Farms, Cal-Organic, Bunny Luv
B	**B+**	HerbThyme, Driscoll's, Pure Pacific, Alexia
	B	Green Giant
	B–	Dole, Ready Pac, Salad Time, Ian's
C	**C+**	Birds Eye, C&W
	C	Ocean Spray, Sun-Maid
	C–	
D	**D+**	Fresh Express
	D	Del Monte
	D–	
F	**F**	Ore-Ida

FRUIT & VEGETABLES

WHAT YOU NEED TO KNOW
Fresh produce is the vanguard of the organic foods movement. It's particularly important to buy local produce, so attend your local farmers' market or join a CSA (community supported agriculture) farm.

BUYING TIPS
✓ Buy organic, locally grown produce

CORPORATE HERO
Earthbound Farm
☆ CAM certified Green Business
☆ Social Venture Network member

CORPORATE VILLAIN
Del Monte
☠ Documented human rights violations
☠ Massive toxic discharge lawsuit

RESOURCES
🖥 www.localharvest.org
🖥 www.ebfarm.com

GASOLINE

A	**A+**	
	A	Sunoco
	A –	BP, Amoco, Arco
B	**B +**	Marathon, Ashland, SuperAmerica
	B	Citgo, 7-Eleven
	B –	Valero, Beacon
C	**C +**	Total, Hess
	C	Shell, Costco
	C –	
D	**D +**	
	D	Conoco, Phillips, 76, JetCoastal
	D –	Chevron, Texaco
F	**F**	Exxon, Mobil

GASOLINE

WHAT YOU NEED TO KNOW

The petroleum industry is one of the least socially and environmentally responsible on the planet, so if you don't want to get your hands dirty, you should sell your car. For the rest of us, it's very important to avoid the companies at the bottom of this category as they are some of the most destructive in existence.

BUYING TIPS

✓ Locate the best ranked gas station near your home and work

CORPORATE HERO

BP-Amoco

☆ Largest solar power manufacturer
☆ Working with Amnesty Int'l & WWF
☆ CER "Best Ethical Ranking" in industry

CORPORATE VILLAIN

Exxon-Mobil

☠ #1 worst corporation on the planet
☠ Renowned human rights violator
☠ #5 in "Top 100 Corporate Criminals"

GUM & MINTS

A	A+	
	A	Glee Gum, Hain
	A–	Speakeasy, St. Claire's
B	B+	
	B	
	B–	Dentyne, Trident, Cinnaburst, Chiclets, Certs, Clorets, Bubblicious
C	C+	Bubble Yum, Breathsavers, Ice Breakers
	C	Air Heads
	C–	
D	D+	
	D	Extra, Eclipse, Orbit, Big Red, Big League Chew, LifeSavers, Wrigley's, Winterfresh, Freedent, Hubba Bubba, Altoids
	D–	
F	F	After Eight

GUM & MINTS

WHAT YOU NEED TO KNOW
The candy industry has a long way to go before we have widely available socially responsible options. When you find them, buy them!

BUYING TIPS
✓ Search for organic gum and mints

CORPORATE HERO

Glee Gum

☆ CAM certified Green Business
☆ Uses wild-harvested rainforest plants
☆ Actively supports environmental orgs.
☆ Provides rainforest education kits

CORPORATE VILLAIN

Orbit (Wrigley's)

☠ CEP "F" for overall social responsibility
☠ Refuses disclosure to consumers

RESOURCES
🖥 www.gleegum.com
🖥 www.aarrgghh.com/cloudninecandy
🖥 www.econaturalsolutions.com

HAIR CARE

A	**A+**	Druide
	A	Aveda
	A−	Jason, Aubrey Organics, Kiss My Face, Burt's Bees, Body Shop
B	**B+**	EO, Nature's Gate, Ecco Bella, Pure & Basic, Paul Mitchell, Pure Essentials
	B	Alba, Avalon, Giovanni, Emerald Forest, Shikai
	B−	Aloe Vera 80
C	**C+**	Head & Shoulders, Pert, Pantene, Clairol, Aussie
	C	White Rain, Citre Shine, Dep, L.A. Looks
	C−	Suave, Finesse, Dove, ThermaSilk
D	**D+**	VO5, Nexxus
	D	
	D−	
F	**F**	L'Oréal, Garnier, Biolage

HAIR CARE

BUYING TIPS
- ✓ Avoid products tested on animals
- ✓ Seek out items made with organic ingredients
- ✓ Look for recyclable containers — #1, #2 plastic
- ✓ Buy larger quantities to reduce packaging

CORPORATE HERO

Druide

- ☆ 100% sustainably harvested ingredients
- ☆ Uses strict ECOCERT organic standards
- ☆ Fair trade, organic ingredients
- ☆ Industry leader in environment category

CORPORATE VILLAIN

Biolage (L'Oreal)

- ☠ Continues unnecessary animal testing
- ☠ Ingredients include known carcinogens
- ☠ Company a target of two major boycotts

RESOURCES
- 🖥 www.druide.ca
- 🖥 www.aveda.com
- 🖥 www.thebodyshop.com
- 🖥 www.aubrey-organics.com

ICE CREAM & ALTERNATIVES

A	**A+**	
	A	Stonyfield Farms, Ben & Jerry's, Soy Delicious, Straus Family
	A–	Celestial Seasonings, Wholesoy, Rice/Soy Dream, Natural Choice
B	**B+**	Double Rainbow, Julie's, Newman's Own
	B	Starbucks
	B–	Dole
C	**C+**	Weight Watchers, Godiva
	C	Tofutti, Crystal, Fruitfull
	C–	Breyers, Klondike
D	**D+**	Dove, Snickers
	D	
	D–	Healthy Choice
F	**F**	Dreyer's, Nestle, Häagen Dazs

ICE CREAM & ALTERNATIVES

BUYING TIPS

✓ Choose ice cream with organic ingredients
✓ Look for fair trade coffee/chocolate flavors

CORPORATE HERO

Ben & Jerry's

☆ Socially responsible business leader
☆ Winner, Sustainability Report Award
☆ CEP "A" for overall social responsibility

CORPORATE VILLAIN

Häagen Dazs (Nestle)

☠ Baby formula human rights boycott
☠ "Most Irresponsible" corporation award
☠ Involved in child slavery lawsuit
☠ Aggressive takeovers of family farms

RESOURCES

🖥 www.benjerry.com
🖥 www.soydelicious.com
🖥 www.stonyfield.com
🖥 www.strausmilk.com

JUICE

A	**A+**	
	A	Cascadian Farm, Horizon
	A−	Santa Cruz Organic, Walnut Acres, Purity, Lakewood
B	**B+**	Newman's Own
	B	Dole, Tropicana, Gatorade
	B−	After The Fall, Odwalla, RW Knudsen, Hawaiian Punch, Mott's
C	**C+**	V8
	C	Welch's, Hawaii's Own, Florida's Natural, L&A, Langers, Ocean Spray, TreeTop, Martinelli's
	C−	
D	**D+**	
	D	Minute Maid
	D−	
F	**F**	Capri Sun, Kool-Aid, Libby's, Kern's

JUICE

BUYING TIPS
- ✓ Purchase organic juices when available
- ✓ Buy juices in aluminum or glass containers
- ✓ #1 or #2 when plastics are the only option
- ✓ Buy larger quantities to reduce packaging

CORPORATE HERO

Cascadian Farm

- ☆ CAM certified Green Business
- ☆ Socially Responsible Business Award
- ☆ Offers complete line of organic products

CORPORATE VILLAIN

Minute Maid (Coke)

- ☠ MM's "Worst Corporation" list for 3 years
- ☠ Hinders clean water access abroad
- ☠ Target of major human rights boycotts

RESOURCES
- 💻 www.cascadianfarm.com
- 💻 www.horizonorganic.com
- 💻 www.walnutacres.com
- 💻 www.newmansown.com
- 💻 www.cokewatch.org

LAUNDRY SUPPLIES

A	**A+**	Seventh Generation
	A	Ecover
	A–	Bi-o-Kleen, ECOS, Earth Friendly, Country Save, Lifetree, Bio Pac, Planet, Oasis, Mountain Green
B	**B+**	Natural Value
	B	
	B–	Shout, Fab, Fresh Start, Dynamo
C	**C+**	Biz, Bold, Downy, Tide, Bounce, Ivory, Febreze, Gain, Era, Cheer
	C	Wisk, Arm & Hammer, All, Snuggle, Surf
	C–	Oxi Clean, Static Guard
D	**D+**	Cling Free, Spray'n Wash, Woolite, Vivid
	D	
	D–	
F	**F**	Clorox, Borax, Purex

For more detailed data visit – www.betterworldshopper.org

LAUNDRY SUPPLIES

BUYING TIPS
✓ Avoid #3 plastic containers — choose #1 or #2
✓ Avoid phosphates and chlorine bleach

CORPORATE HERO

Ecover

☆ CAM certified Green Business
☆ Winner, environmental leader award
☆ UN Global 500 Environment Honor Roll
☆ 1st truly ecological factory in the world

CORPORATE VILLAIN

Clorox

☠ On MM's "10 Worst Corporations" list
☠ Continues unnecessary animal testing
☠ Refuses disclosure to consumers
☠ Major producer of chlorine — dioxin

RESOURCES
🖳 www.seventhgen.com
🖳 www.ecover.com
🖳 www.ecos.com
🖳 www.planetinc.com
🖳 www.bi-o-kleen.com

MEAT ALTERNATIVES

A	**A+**	White Wave, TofuTown
	A	Amy's, Wildwood
	A−	Yves, Small Planet
B	**B+**	Turtle Island, Tofurkey, SuperBurgers
	B	
	B−	Morningstar Farms
C	**C+**	Pete's
	C	Gardenburger, Veggie Patch, Veat, Soy Deli, Health Is Wealth, Sweet Earth, Mori-Nu, Nasoya, Vitasoy, Primal Strips
	C−	Quorn
D	**D+**	
	D	Lightlife
	D−	
F	**F**	Boca

MEAT ALTERNATIVES

WHAT YOU NEED TO KNOW

Meat alternatives have come a long way since the days of tofu jokes. Burgers, hot dogs, chicken strips, lunch meat, and more are now convincingly tasty in vegetarian form and tend to have a smaller ecological footprint than their counterparts.

CORPORATE HERO

White Wave

☆ Actively supports small, family farms
☆ Powered by 100% renewable energy
☆ EPA "Green Partner Of The Year"

CORPORATE VILLAIN

Boca (Altria)

☠ MM's "Worst Corporation" list for 5 years
☠ Greenwash Award for public deception
☠ Spent over $100 million on lobbyists

RESOURCES

💻 www.whitewave.com
💻 www.tofurkey.com

MEAT PRODUCTS

A	**A+**	
	A	Organic Prairie
	A−	Shelton's, MBA Brand, Coleman, Niman Ranch, Diestel
B	**B+**	
	B	
	B−	Hillshire Farm, Ball Park, Jimmy Dean
C	**C+**	
	C	Foster Farms, Valley Fresh, Hickory Farms
	C−	
D	**D+**	Hormel, Farmer John, Jennie-O, SPAM
	D	Banquet, Butterball, Libby's, Healthy Choice, Eckrich, Armour, Slim Jim, Hebrew National
	D−	Tyson
F	**F**	Oscar Mayer, Louis Rich

MEAT PRODUCTS

WHAT YOU NEED TO KNOW

Meat production tends to consume more resources than agriculture, so it's especially important to choose sustainable, humane options.

BUYING TIPS

✓ Choose free-range, organic meat options

CORPORATE HERO

Organic Prairie

☆ Small family farmer-owned co-operative
☆ Gives 10% of profits to local community
☆ Humane animal treatment a priority

CORPORATE VILLAIN

Tyson Foods

☠ MM's "Worst Corporation" list for 2 years
☠ CEP "F" for overall social responsibility
☠ Guilty of 20+ violations of Clean Air Act

RESOURCES

🖥 www.organicprairie.com
🖥 www.smartchicken.com
🖥 www.colemannatural.com

MEDICAL

A	**A+**	
	A	
	A–	
B	**B+**	Johnson & Johnson, McNeil
	B	3M, Bristol-Myers Squibb
	B–	Merck
C	**C+**	Procter & Gamble, Halls, Cadbury Adams, Novartis, Bausch & Lomb
	C	Chattem Chemicals, Insight
	C–	
D	**D+**	Schering-Plough
	D	GlaxoSmithKline
	D–	Bayer
F	**F**	Wyeth, Pfizer, Whitehall-Robins, Pharmacia

MEDICAL

WHAT YOU NEED TO KNOW

Pharmaceutical companies are some of the most powerful and least responsible of any on the planet. When you do have a choice of medical products, it is very important that you choose the better companies.

BUYING TIPS

✓ Make sure to look on the back of the box to see what company manufactures an item

CORPORATE HERO

Johnson & Johnson

☆ On CK's "100 Most Sustainable" list
☆ EPA Green Power Leader award winner
☆ CEP "A" for overall social responsibility
☆ Business Ethics Award winner

CORPORATE VILLAIN

Wyeth

☠ MM's "Worst Corporation" list for 2 years
☠ Target of major animal welfare boycott
☠ Numerous federal ethics violations
☠ Responsible for EPA Superfund site

MILK & ALTERNATIVES

A	**A+**	Silk, Straus Family, Edensoy
	A	Horizon
	A–	Organic Valley, Nancy's, Organic Pastures, WestSoy, Rice/Soy Dream, AmaZake, Helios
B	**B+**	Clover Stornetta, Pacific
	B	Lactaid
	B–	8th Continent
C	**C+**	Alta Dena
	C	Crystal, Vitasoy
	C–	
D	**D+**	
	D	
	D–	Nestle
F	**F**	Knudsen

MILK & ALTERNATIVES

WHAT YOU NEED TO KNOW

Now there are a wide range of socially responsible options for both dairy and non-dairy milk lovers.

CORPORATE HERO

Silk (White Wave)

☆ Actively supports small, family farms
☆ Powered by 100% renewable energy
☆ Industry environmental leader
☆ EPA "Green Partner Of The Year"

CORPORATE HERO

Straus Family

☆ 1st 100% organic dairy in US
☆ Uses returnable glass bottles for milk
☆ Utilizes methane capture for waste
☆ Small, sustainable family farm

RESOURCES

🖥 www.silksoymilk.com
🖥 www.strausmilk.com
🖥 www.edenfoods.com

OFFICE SUPPLIES

A	**A+**	
	A	
	A–	HP, IBM
B	**B+**	Herman Miller, Pitney Bowes, Xerox
	B	FedEx, Kinko's, Ricoh, Canon
	B–	Imation, 3M, Scotch
C	**C+**	Staples, UPS, Epson, IKON, Brother
	C	Zebra, Crayola, Fiskar, Elmer's, Sharpie, Expo, Bic, Parker, Pentel, Papermate, Uniball, Pilot, Sanford
	C–	
D	**D+**	Rubbermaid, Airborne Express
	D	OfficeMax, Avery
	D–	Office Depot, BASF
F	**F**	Smurfit-Stone Container

OFFICE SUPPLIES

WHAT YOU NEED TO KNOW
Many of the items we use during the day are in some way related to our workplace. If you have any potential influence over office purchasing, consider suggesting a shift in funds over to more socially responsible products.

CORPORATE HERO
Hewlett Packard

☆ Free return recycling of its computers
☆ Perfect 100 on HRC Equality Index
☆ Countless awards for business ethics

CORPORATE VILLAIN
Smurfit-Stone

☠ On MM's "10 Worst Corporations" list
☠ Illegal pollution dumping cover-ups
☠ Fatal worker safety violations
☠ EPA top toxic waste producer
☠ Worst environmental record in industry

RESOURCES
🖥 www.hp.com
🖥 www.ibm.com

OIL & VINEGAR

A	**A+**	Eden Foods, Rapunzel
	A	Spectrum, Hain, Hollywood
	A–	Napa Valley Naturals
B	**B+**	Earth Balance, Natural Value
	B	Nutiva, Mazola
	B–	Bragg, Crisco, BioNature
C	**C+**	Sagra
	C	Star, Canola Harvest, Saffola, Nakano
	C–	Bertolli
D	**D+**	Heinz
	D	
	D–	
F	**F**	Wesson, Pam

OIL & VINEGAR

WHAT YOU NEED TO KNOW

A number of socially responsible companies now offer conventional and organic oils and vinegars.

BUYING TIPS

✓ Choose organic oil, vinegar & cooking spray

CORPORATE HERO

Spectrum

☆ Uses eco-certification for international suppliers
☆ Partners with international worker co-ops
☆ Promotes small-scale, sustainable farms

CORPORATE VILLAIN

Pam (Altria)

☣ Greenwash Award for public deception
☣ Undermines overseas health standards
☣ Spent over $100 million on lobbyists
☣ MM's "Worst Corporation" list for 5 years

RESOURCES

🖥 www.rapunzel.com
🖥 www.edenfoods.com
🖥 www.spectrumorganics.com

OLIVES & PICKLES

A	**A+**	
	A	Cascadian Farm
	A–	Mediterranean Organic
B	**B+**	Santa Barbara, Natural Value
	B	
	B–	Mt. Olive
C	**C+**	Bubbies, Minasso
	C	Star, Mezzetta, Lindsay, Early California, Vlasic, Armstrong, Tassos
	C–	
D	**D+**	Del Monte
	D	
	D–	
F	**F**	Claussen

OLIVES & PICKLES

WHAT YOU NEED TO KNOW

Organic varieties of olives and pickles are just beginning to become available for consumers.

BUYING TIPS

✓ Buy larger quantities to reduce packaging
✓ Purchase organic olives & pickles

CORPORATE HERO

Cascadian Farm

☆ CAM certified Green Business
☆ Socially Responsible Business Award
☆ Offers complete line of organic products

CORPORATE VILLAIN

Claussen (Altria)

☠ Part of #2 worst company on the earth
☠ Currently the target of 2 major boycotts
☠ Named "Top 10 Greenwasher"

RESOURCES

💻 www.cascadianfarm.com
💻 www.mediterraneanorganic.com
💻 www.sbolive.com

PAPER

A	**A+**	
	A	New Leaf, Living Tree
	A–	
B	**B+**	HP, IBM
	B	Kodak, Xerox
	B–	3M, Canon, Kinko's
C	**C+**	Great White, Hammermill
	C	Epson
	C–	Staples
D	**D+**	Boise Cascade, Avery, OfficeMax
	D	Office Depot
	D–	Georgia-Pacific
F	**F**	Mead

PAPER

WHAT YOU NEED TO KNOW
Just remember one thing: PAPER = TREES.

BUYING TIPS
✓ Look for high post-consumer recycled
   content
✓ Choose non-chlorine bleached paper options
✓ New Leaf paper is now at Kinko's — ask for it

CORPORATE HERO

New Leaf

☆ Forest Stewardship Council certified
☆ Offers 100% post-consumer options
☆ Invented the Eco-Audit for books, etc.
☆ Uses sustainably harvested wood

CORPORATE VILLAIN

Mead-Westvaco

☠ Low score on HRC Equality Index
☠ Continues unnecessary animal testing
☠ Refuses disclosure to consumers
☠ Named global climate change laggard

RESOURCES
🖥 www.newleafpaper.com

PAPER TOWELS & TOILET PAPER

A	**A+**	Seventh Generation
	A	Earth Friendly
	A–	Marcal
B	**B+**	Natural Value
	B	Green Forest
	B–	Kleenex, Viva, Scott, Cottonelle
C	**C+**	Bounty, Puffs, Charmin
	C	
	C–	
D	**D+**	Softly
	D	
	D–	
F	**F**	Quilted Northern, Angel Soft, Brawny, Sparkle

PAPER TOWELS & TOILET PAPER

WHAT YOU NEED TO KNOW
You can make a lot of difference for our global forests by choosing these two items in a responsible manner.

BUYING TIPS
✓ Look for high post-consumer recycled content
✓ Choose non-chlorine bleached paper options
✓ Always buy items with some recycled content

CORPORATE HERO
Seventh Generation
☆ Ranked #1 best company on the planet
☆ Empowers consumers w/packaging
☆ Winner, Sustainability Report Award
☆ Socially Responsible Business Award

CORPORATE VILLAIN
Brawny (Georgia-Pacific)
☠ #44 in "Top 100 Corporate Criminals"
☠ Massive toxic PCB dumping fines
☠ Named global climate change laggard

PASTA & SAUCE

A	**A+**	Eden Foods
	A	Muir Glen, Annie's
	A–	DeBoles, Newman's Own
B	**B+**	Hodgson Mill
	B	Golden Grain
	B–	
C	**C+**	Prego
	C	Barilla, Ronzoni, Stella, Emeril's, McCormick, American Beauty, De Cecco
	C–	Ragu, Bertolli, Knorr, Lawry's
D	**D+**	Contadina, Classico
	D	
	D–	Chef Boyardee, Hunt's
F	**F**	Kraft, Buitoni

PASTA & SAUCE

BUYING TIPS
- ✓ Look for items made with organic ingredients
- ✓ Buy larger quantities to reduce packaging

CORPORATE HERO

Annie's

- ☆ Regularly donates products to nonprofits
- ☆ Created environmental studies scholarship
- ☆ Supports organic, family farms
- ☆ CAM certified Green Business

CORPORATE VILLAIN

Kraft (Altria)

- ☻ #1 contributor to Washington lobbyists
- ☻ Greenwash Award for public deception
- ☻ Undermines overseas health standards
- ☻ Part of #2 worst company on the earth

RESOURCES
- 💻 www.annies.com
- 💻 www.muirglen.com
- 💻 www.deboles.com
- 💻 www.newmansown.com
- 💻 www.hodgsonmill.com

PEANUT BUTTER & JELLY

A	A+	Kettle Foods
	A	Cascadian Farm, Maranatha
	A–	Woodstock Farms, Arrowhead Mills
B	B+	
	B	
	B–	Adam's, Jif, Laura Scudder, Mary Ellen, Smucker's
C	C+	Sorrell Ridge, Bonne Maman
	C	Welch's
	C–	Skippy
D	D+	
	D	
	D–	
F	F	Peter Pan, Knott's

PEANUT BUTTER & JELLY

BUYING TIPS
✓ Look for items made with organic ingredients
✓ Buy larger quantities to reduce packaging

CORPORATE HERO

Kettle Foods

☆ 100% of waste oil turned into biodiesel
☆ Restored local wetlands habitat
☆ One of the largest solar arrays in Northwest US
☆ Gives tons of potatoes to hunger orgs

CORPORATE VILLAIN

Peter Pan (ConAgra)

☙ Food industry "Climate Change Laggard"
☙ #50 in "Top 100 Corporate Criminals"
☙ 2nd largest E. coli meat recall in history
☙ Many worker safety & health violations

RESOURCES
⌨ www.kettlefoods.com
⌨ www.cascadianfarm.com
⌨ www.maranathanutbutters.com

PET CARE

A	**A+**	
	A	
	A–	Newman's Own Organic, PetGuard, Swheat Scoop, Health Valley, Feline Pine
B	**B+**	Natural Value, Natural Life
	B	Heartland, Innova, Nutro, Sensible Choice, Avoderm
	B–	Science Diet
C	**C+**	IAMS
	C	Hartz, Jonny Cat, Cat's Pride, Arm & Hammer
	C–	
D	**D+**	Whiskas, Sheba
	D	9 Lives, Kibbles 'n Bits, Pedigree, Del Monte
	D–	Fresh Step, Scoop Away
F	**F**	Purina, Meow Mix, Alpo, Fancy Feast, ONE, Friskies, Milk-Bone

PET CARE

WHAT YOU NEED TO KNOW
Recent innovations have been made in the area of socially responsible pet care, so you should have a number of excellent options to choose from.

BUYING TIPS
✓ Buy pet food made with organic ingredients
✓ Buy cat litter made from renewable sources

CORPORATE HERO

Newman's Own

☆ 100% of profits to education & charity
☆ CEP "A" for overall social responsibility
☆ Has given over $200 million to good causes

CORPORATE VILLAIN

Purina (Nestle)

☠ "Most Irresponsible" corporation award
☠ Aggressive takeovers of family farms
☠ Involved in child slavery lawsuit

RESOURCES
🖥 www.felinepine.com
🖥 www.swheatscoop.com

PIZZA

A	**A+**	
	A	Amy's
	A−	American Flatbread
B	**B+**	
	B	Totino's
	B−	
C	**C+**	
	C	Celeste, Red Baron, Freschetta, Tony's
	C−	Bravissimo
D	**D+**	
	D	Linda McCartney
	D−	
F	**F**	Stouffer's, Tombstone, Boca, DiGiorno, California Pizza Kitchen

PIZZA

WHAT YOU NEED TO KNOW
One of the most popular items in the frozen
food aisle, consumers still have a very limited
selection of socially responsible options.

BUYING TIPS
✓ Buy pizza made with organic ingredients

CORPORATE HERO

Amy's Kitchen

☆ Donates food to relief efforts
☆ Produces all-vegetarian, organic foods
☆ CAM certified Green Business

CORPORATE VILLAIN

Tombstone (Altria)

☠ MM's "Worst Corporation" list for 5 years
☠ Greenwash Award for public deception
☠ Spent over $100 million on lobbyists
☠ Involved in document deletion cover-up

RESOURCES
🖥 www.amyskitchen.com
🖥 www.americanflatbread.com

POPCORN, NUTS & PRETZELS

A	**A+**	
	A	
	A−	Newman's Own Organic, Woodstock Farms, Hain, Bearitos
B	**B+**	Snyder's
	B	Pop Secret, Gardetto's, Chex Mix
	B−	Rold Gold, Smartfood
C	**C+**	
	C	Jolly Time, ExpresSnacks
	C−	
D	**D+**	Blue Diamond
	D	
	D−	Act II, Crunch 'n Munch, Orville Redenbacher, David, Jiffy Pop
F	**F**	Planters, Corn Nuts

POPCORN, NUTS & PRETZELS

WHAT YOU NEED TO KNOW
When you're settling in to watch a little TV or a movie, what you put in that bowl next to the couch makes a big difference for the planet.

BUYING TIPS
✓ Look for items made with organic ingredients

CORPORATE HERO
Newman's Own

☆ 100% of profits to education & charity
☆ CEP "A" for overall social responsibility
☆ Has given over $200 million to good causes

CORPORATE VILLAIN
Planters (Altria)

☠ Part of #2 worst company on the earth
☠ Currently the target of 2 major boycotts
☠ #1 contributor to Washington lobbyists

RESOURCES
🖥 www.newmansownorganics.com

RETAIL STORES

A	**A+**	Patagonia
	A	
	A–	IKEA, REI
B	**B+**	
	B	L.L. Bean
	B–	Home Depot
C	**C+**	Target, Eddie Bauer
	C	
	C–	BJ's, Best Buy
D	**D+**	JC Penney, Walgreens
	D	Maytag, Costco, Sears
	D–	Rite Aid, Kmart
F	**F**	Wal-Mart, Sam's Club

RETAIL STORES

CORPORATE HERO

Patagonia

☆ Environmental leader in industry
☆ Plastic bottles recycling pioneer — fleece
☆ 1% of sales goes to enviro groups
☆ Powered by 100% renewable energy

CORPORATE HERO

IKEA

☆ Works with UNICEF & Greenpeace
☆ Uses no timber from natural forests
☆ Involved in affordable housing efforts
☆ Supports efforts to stop international child labor

CORPORATE VILLAIN

Wal-Mart

☠ #3 worst company on the planet
☠ CEP "F" for overall social responsibility
☠ Sex-discrimination class-action lawsuit
☠ Documented exploitation of child labor

RESOURCES

🖥 www.patagonia.com
🖥 www.ikea.com
🖥 www.rei.com

RICE &
OTHER GRAINS

A	**A+**	Eden Foods
	A	Fantastic Foods
	A−	Near East, Lundberg, Seeds Of Change
B	**B+**	Betty Crocker
	B	Rice-A-Roni
	B−	
C	**C+**	
	C	Carolina, Goya, S&W, Mahatma, Success Rice, Manischewitz
	C−	
D	**D+**	Lipton, Uncle Ben's
	D	
	D−	
F	**F**	Minute Rice, Kraft

RICE & OTHER GRAINS

BUYING TIPS

✓ Look for organic grains
✓ Buy in bulk to reduce packaging waste

CORPORATE HERO

Eden Foods

☆ Ranked #8 best company on the planet
☆ CEP's highest social responsibility score
☆ CAM certified Green Business
☆ Environmental leader in food industry

CORPORATE VILLAIN

Minute Rice (Altria)

☠ MM's "Worst Corporation" list for 5 years
☠ Greenwash Award for public deception
☠ Spent over $100 million on lobbyists
☠ Involved in document deletion cover-up

RESOURCES

🖳 www.edenfoods.com
🖳 www.fantasticfoods.com
🖳 www.seedsofchange.com

SALAD DRESSING

A	**A+**	
	A	Spectrum, Follow Your Heart, Annie's Naturals
	A−	
B	**B+**	Newman's Own, Drew's
	B	
	B−	
C	**C+**	Pepperidge Farm
	C	Brianna's, Marie's, Mrs. Cubbison's, Cardini's, Girard's, Ken's Steak House
	C−	Bernstein's, Wish-Bone
D	**D+**	
	D	Hidden Valley
	D−	
F	**F**	Kraft, Good Seasons

SALAD DRESSING

WHAT YOU NEED TO KNOW
While there are still only a handful of socially responsible companies in this category, they offer a wide variety of salad dressings.

BUYING TIPS
✓ Buy dressing made with organic ingredients

CORPORATE HERO

Spectrum

☆ Uses eco-certification for int'l suppliers
☆ Partners with int'l worker co-ops
☆ Promotes small-scale, sustainable farms

CORPORATE VILLAIN

Kraft (Altria)

☠ Part of #2 worst company on the earth
☠ Named global climate change laggard
☠ Undermines overseas health standards

RESOURCES
🖥 www.spectrumorganics.com
🖥 www.anniesnaturals.com
🖥 www.followyourheart.com

SALSA, SPREADS & DIPS

A	**A+**	
	A	Emerald Valley, Muir Glen, Wildwood
	A–	Walnut Acres, Bearitos, Rising Moon, Seeds Of Change
B	**B+**	Newman's Own
	B	
	B–	Tostitos
C	**C+**	Pace
	C	Casa Sanchez, Nonna Lena's, Micaela's, Affi's, Raquel's, Frontera
	C–	
D	**D+**	La Victoria, Ortega
	D	
	D–	
F	**F**	Taco Bell

SALSA, SPREADS & DIPS

WHAT YOU NEED TO KNOW
This category includes everything from hummus to salsa to bean dip, and there are responsible choices to be had for every one.

CORPORATE HERO

Emerald Valley

☆ Socially Responsible Business Award
☆ 1% to humanitarian & ecological causes
☆ Green Business Of The Year Award

CORPORATE VILLAIN

Taco Bell (Altria)

☠ Named "Top 10 Greenwasher"
☠ Involved in document deletion cover-up
☠ Continues to do business in Burma
☠ Spent over $100 million on lobbyists

RESOURCES
🖥 www.emeraldvalleykitchen.com
🖥 www.muirglen.com
🖥 www.seedsofchange.com

SEAFOOD I

A	**A+**	EcoFish
	A	Wildcatch
	A–	Natural Sea
B	**B+**	
	B	Contessa, Bela, Natural Value
	B–	
C	**C+**	Omega Foods, Crown Prince
	C	Flott, Deep Sea, Chicken of the Sea, Bumble Bee, King Oscar, Beach Cliff, Van de Kamp's, Lasco, Geisha, Yankee Clipper, Snow's, Brunswick, Vince's, Star, Gorton's
	C–	
D	**D+**	Starkist
	D	
	D–	
F	**F**	Louis Kemp

SEAFOOD I

WHAT YOU NEED TO KNOW
One of the most important changes you can make is in choosing ecologically responsible seafood.

BUYING TIPS
✓ Look for labels evidencing sustainable fishing
✓ Local freshwater is often a good choice
✓ See next section for more seafood guidance

CORPORATE HERO
Eco Fish

☆ Only environmentally sustainable fishing
☆ Conservation scientists advisory board
☆ Result of marine conservation groups

CORPORATE VILLAIN
Louis Kemp (ConAgra)

☠ MM's "Worst Corporation" list for 2 years
☠ Food industry "Climate Change Laggard"
☠ Many worker safety & health violations

RESOURCES
⌨ www.ecofish.com
⌨ www.wildcatch.com

SEAFOOD II

A	A+	Mussels, Clams, Anchovies, Wild Salmon, Mackerel, Tilapia, Herring, Sardines, Striped Bass, Catfish
B	B+	Oysters, Snow Crab, Stone Crab, Trout, Pacific Cod, Pacific Halibut, Mahi-mahi, Alaskan Halibut
C	C+	Scallops, Prawns, Squid, Tuna, King Crab, Blue Crab, Imitation Crab, Lingcod, Bluefish, Lobster, Dogfish
D	D+	Sole, Shrimp, Eel, Caviar, Swordfish, Flounder, Rockfish, Sea Bass, Haddock
F	F	Shark, Roughy, Marlin, Red Snapper, Atlantic Cod, Atlantic Halibut, Farmed & Atlantic Salmon, Grouper

SEAFOOD II

WHAT YOU NEED TO KNOW
Our current fishing practices are destroying
ocean life at an unprecedented rate. Rather
than ranking companies, the chart to the left
shows which species are being more sustainably harvested and which are being fished out
of existence. It also takes into account the
environmental costs of harvesting each kind
of seafood. Use it at both the supermarket
seafood counter and when you go out to eat.

BUYING TIPS
✓ When its unclear, ask the deli staffer or server
  for more specifics about the fish
✓ When A or B category seafood is not available, consider non-seafood alternatives

RESOURCES
🖥 www.mbayaq.org/cr/seafoodwatch.asp
🖥 www.seafoodwatch.org
🖥 www.oceansalive.org/eat.cfm
🖥 www.blueocean.org/seafood

SHOES

A	**A+**	Ecolution, Blackspot, No Sweat
	A	Earth Shoes
	A–	Birkenstock
B	**B+**	Timberland
	B	Reebok
	B–	Nike
C	**C+**	Adidas, Puma
	C	
	C–	New Balance
D	**D+**	K-Swiss, Stride Rite
	D	Converse, Florsheim, Fortune, Vans, Saucony, Skechers
	D–	LA Gear
F	**F**	DISCOUNT & DEPARTMENT STORE BRANDS

SHOES

WHAT YOU NEED TO KNOW

Almost all store-bought shoes are made in factories in the developing world. The real question is: how are the workers treated, are they safe, and do they make enough of a wage to live decently? Your choices here will determine the answers to those questions for thousands.

CORPORATE HERO

Ecolution

☆ CAM certified Green Business
☆ "Top Rung", Ladder of Responsibility
☆ Utilizes eco-friendly hemp in its shoes

CORPORATE VILLAIN

LA Gear

☠ Named "Sweatshop Laggard"
☠ CEP "F" for overall social responsibility
☠ No supplier code of conduct for workers

RESOURCES

🖥 www.earth.us
🖥 www.ecolution.com
🖥 www.blackspotsneaker.org

SOAP

A	**A+**	
	A	Dr. Bronner's, Tom's of Maine
	A–	Jäsön, Burt's Bees, Aubrey Organics, Kiss My Face, Simmons
B	**B+**	Sappo Hill, River Soap, Plantlife, Zum Bar
	B	EO, Alba, Avalon, Shikai
	B–	Clearly Natural
C	**C+**	Zest, Softsoap, Ivory, Irish Spring, Safeguard, Olay
	C	Rainbow
	C–	Dove, Suave, Caress, Lever 2000
D	**D+**	Dial, Coast, Tone
	D	
	D–	
F	**F**	Purell

SOAP

BUYING TIPS
✓ Choose soaps that aren't tested on animals
✓ Buy soaps with less or recyclable packaging

CORPORATE HERO

Dr. Bronner's

☆ Leader in organic standards integrity
☆ 5:1 CEO to worker salary cap
☆ Profits donated to variety of causes
☆ Liquid soaps in 100% recycled plastic
☆ Does not test on animals

CORPORATE VILLAIN

Dial

☠ Continues unnecessary animal testing
☠ CEP "F" for overall social responsibility
☠ Refuses disclosure to consumers
☠ Sexual discrimination/harassment suits

RESOURCES
💻 www.drbronner.com
💻 www.tomsofmaine.com
💻 www.aubreyorganics.com
💻 www.kissmyface.com

SODA

A	**A+**	
	A	Santa Cruz Organic, Bossa Nova, Steaz
	A −	Reed's, Virgil's
B	**B+**	Blue Sky, Hansen's, Newman's Own
	B	Sierra Mist, Tropicana, Mug, Pepsi, Mountain Dew, Slice
	B −	Lipton
C	**C +**	Canada Dry, Crush, IBC, Diet Rite, Orangina, 7-Up, Snapple, Squirt, Sunkist, Welch's, A&W, Stewart's, Schweppes, Dr Pepper
	C	
	C −	
D	**D+**	
	D	Minute Maid, Coca-Cola, Pibb Xtra, Sprite, Fanta, Barq's
	D −	
F	**F**	Country Time

SODA

WHAT YOU NEED TO KNOW
If you're like most people, soda is a daily part of your diet. Move up on the responsible soda chain to avoid companies that are wrecking the planet.

BUYING TIPS
✓ Buy soda in aluminum or glass containers

CORPORATE HERO

Steaz

☆ Organic drinks industry leader
☆ Profits donated to Sri Lankan village
☆ Supports sustainable farming practices

CORPORATE VILLAIN

Coca-Cola

☠ MM's "Worst Corporation" list for 3 years
☠ Hinders clean water access abroad
☠ Target of major human rights boycotts

RESOURCES
🖥 www.steaz.com
🖥 www.bossausa.org
🖥 www.reedsgingerbrew.com

SOUP & NOODLES

A	A+	Rapunzel
	A	Fantastic Foods, Spice Hunter, Amy's, Muir Glen
	A–	Walnut Acres, Imagine, Casbah, Health Valley, Nile Spice
B	B+	Dr. McDougal's
	B	Progresso
	B–	
C	C+	Campbell's
	C	Bear Creek, Maruchan, Nissin, Swanson
	C–	Knorr, Lipton
D	D+	
	D	Herb Ox
	D–	
F	F	Healthy Choice, Wolfgang Puck

SOUP & NOODLES

WHAT YOU NEED TO KNOW
Whether it's instant noodles or pea soup, there are many excellent choices for hot, steaming, socially responsible meals.

BUYING TIPS
✓ Look for soups made with organic ingredients

CORPORATE HERO

Rapunzel

☆ Fair trade & organic leader in food ind.
☆ Supports global sustainable farming
☆ Produced 1st 100% organic chocolate

CORPORATE VILLAIN

Healthy Choice (ConAgra)

☠ Food industry "Climate Change Laggard"
☠ MM's "Worst Corporation" list for 2 years
☠ #50 in "Top 100 Corporate Criminals"

RESOURCES
💻 www.rapunzel.com
💻 www.fantasticfoods.com
💻 www.amyskitchen.com

SUGAR, SPICES & SWEETENERS

A	**A+**	Wholesome Sweeteners, Eden Foods
	A	Frontier, Simply Organic
	A–	Hain, Florida Crystals, Shady Maple Farm
B	**B+**	
	B	Splenda, Spice Islands
	B–	
C	**C+**	Grandma's
	C	C&H, Equal, SugarTwin, Sue Bee, Busy Bee, Mrs. Dash, Butter Buds, Molly McButter, Accent, Sweet 'N Low, McCormick
	C–	Lawry's, Adolph's
D	**D+**	Morton
	D	Hormel
	D–	
F	**F**	

SUGAR, SPICES & SWEETENERS

WHAT YOU NEED TO KNOW
Many of these items we buy once and keep using for years. If you want to make a difference while saving your budget, start here.

BUYING TIPS
✓ Buy in bulk to reduce packaging waste

CORPORATE HERO

Wholesome Sweeteners

☆ 1st US fair trade certified sugar available
☆ Actively supports sustainable farming
☆ Makes a full line of organic sweeteners

CORPORATE VILLAIN

Hormel

☠ Supports inhumane factory farming
☠ Low score on HRC Equality Index

RESOURCES
🖳 www.wholesomesweeteners.com
🖳 www.frontiercoop.com

SUPERMARKETS

A	**A+**	FOOD CO-OPS, FARMERS MARKETS
	A	Whole Foods, Wild Oats
	A−	Trader Joe's
B	**B+**	
	B	A&P
	B−	
C	**C+**	Target, Giant Food, Super G, Stop N Shop
	C	SuperValu, Max Foods, Super Saver, Albertsons, Osco, Save-On, Lucky's, Thriftway
	C−	Safeway, Vons
D	**D+**	Shop 'n Save, Meijer, Food 4 Less, King Soopers, Ralphs, Food Lion
	D	Publix, Costco
	D−	Winn-Dixie, Kmart
F	**F**	Wal-Mart

SUPERMARKETS

WHAT YOU NEED TO KNOW
If you have a choice, changing where you shop is an incredibly powerful action that will support people and the planet above profit.

CORPORATE HERO
Whole Foods

☆ BE's "Best Corporations" list for 3 years
☆ Powered by 100% renewable energy
☆ Business Ethics Award winner
☆ Established animal & poverty foundation
☆ Created animal compassion standards

CORPORATE VILLAIN
Wal-Mart

☠ MM's "Worst Corporation" list for 3 years
☠ Major toxic waste dumping fines
☠ CEP "F" for overall social responsibility
☠ Documented exploitation of child labor
☠ #3 worst company on the planet

RESOURCES
Food co-ops & farmers' markets
🖳 www.localharvest.org
🖳 www.wholefoods.com

TEA

A	**A+**	Honest Tea, Tao Of Tea, Traditional Medicinals, Equal Exchange, Choice
	A	Numi, Zhena's Gypsy, Guayaki
	A–	Republic Of Tea
B	**B+**	Sweet Leaf, Yogi, Tazo, Celestial Seasonings, Oregon Chai
	B	Tetley, Twinings
	B–	Stash
C	**C+**	Bigelow
	C	AriZona, Alvita, Good Earth
	C–	
D	**D+**	Lipton
	D	
	D–	
F	**F**	Nestea

TEA

WHAT YOU NEED TO KNOW
If you drink tea, you have an incredible selection of human and planet friendly varieties to pick from.

BUYING TIPS
✓ Look first and foremost for the fair trade label

CORPORATE HERO
Equal Exchange
☆ CAM certified Green Business
☆ Business Ethics Award winner
☆ Industry leader in fair trade movement

CORPORATE VILLAIN
Nestea (Nestle)
☨ "Most Irresponsible" corporation award
☨ Aggressive takeovers of family farms
☨ Involved in child slavery lawsuit

RESOURCES
⌨ www.equalexchange.com
⌨ www.taooftea.com
⌨ www.honesttea.com
⌨ www.traditionalmedicinals.com

VITAMINS

A	A+	
	A	
	A–	New Chapter, NOW
B	B+	Rainbow Light
	B	
	B–	Nature's Way
C	C+	Natural Factors
	C	Nature's Life, Solaray, VegiLife, Natrol, SuperNutrition, All One, Nature Made, Twinlab, Emergen-C, Country Life, Nature's Plus
	C–	
D	D+	
	D	One-A-Day
	D–	
F	F	Centrum

VITAMINS

BUYING TIPS
✓ Look for organic ingredients in supplements
✓ Buy in recyclable bottles: #1, #2, or glass
✓ Purchase in bulk to reduce packaging waste

CORPORATE HERO

NOW

☆ Reduced waste by 50% in 3 years
☆ Donates to WWF & Second Harvest
☆ Environmental & Sustainability Award
☆ Industry leader in recycling efforts

CORPORATE VILLAIN

Centrum (Wyeth)

☠ MM's "Worst Corporation" list for 2 years
☠ Target of major animal welfare boycott
☠ Numerous federal ethics violations
☠ Responsible for EPA Superfund site
☠ #93 in "Top 100 Corporate Criminals"

RESOURCES
🖥 www.new-chapter.com
🖥 www.nowfoods.com
🖥 www.rainbowlight.com

WATER

A	**A+**	TAP / FILTERED
	A	Biota
	A–	Ethos
B	**B+**	Trinity
	B	Crystal Geyser
	B–	Aquafina, Essentia
C	**C+**	
	C	Fiji, La Croix, Hawaii, Glaceau
	C–	
D	**D+**	Crystal Springs, Dannon, Evian, Volvic
	D	Dasani
	D–	
F	**F**	Arrowhead, Calistoga, Perrier, S. Pellegrino, Vittel, Poland Spring, Deer Park, Zephyr Hills, Ozarka, Ice Mountain

WATER

BUYING TIPS
- ✓ Carry your own reusable bottle
- ✓ Buy fewer, larger bottles, and refill them
- ✓ ALWAYS recycle the bottles when done

CORPORATE HERO

Ethos

- ☆ Every bottle sold = donation to clean water projects in the developing world
- ☆ Only third-world-friendly bottled water

CORPORATE HERO

Biota

- ☆ World's 1st compostable bottles — corn
- ☆ Only eco-friendly bottled water

CORPORATE VILLAIN

Arrowhead (Nestle)

- ☠ "Most Irresponsible" corporation award
- ☠ Baby formula human rights boycott

RESOURCES
- 💻 www.biotaspringwater.com
- 💻 www.ethoswater.com
- 💻 www.trinitysprings.com

WINE

A	**A+**	LOCAL VINEYARDS
	A	Banrock Station, Frey, Fetzer
	A−	Great White Wines, Lolonis
B	**B+**	Sobon Estate
	B	
	B−	Yellow Tail, Gallo, Burlwood, Copperidge
C	**C+**	Beringer, Stone Cellar
	C	Inglenook, Woodbridge, Kendall-Jackson, Sutter Home, Franzia, Glen Ellen, Carlo Rossi, Lindemans
	C−	
D	**D+**	
	D	Sterling
	D−	
F	**F**	Clos Du Bois, Jacob's Creek

For more detailed data visit – www.betterworldshopper.org

WINE

BUYING TIPS

✓ Look for organic wine varieties on the shelf
✓ Support local vineyards — try their wine
✓ Buy in bulk to reduce packaging waste

CORPORATE HERO

Fetzer

☆ Powered by 100% renewable energy
☆ All vineyards certified organic
☆ Reduced production waste by 94%
☆ Bottles are 40% recycled glass
☆ BE Award for Environmental Excellence

CORPORATE VILLAIN

Clos Du Bois (Fortune)

☒ CEP "F" for overall social responsibility
☒ No supplier code of conduct for workers
☒ Named "Sweatshop Laggard"
☒ Rated "Poor" by EC

RESOURCES

🖥 www.fetzer.com
🖥 www.freywine.com
🖥 www.banrockstation.com

PRODUCT CATEGORY INDEX

CAN'T FIND...	LOOK UNDER...
Antiperspirant	Body Care
Apple Sauce	Canned Fruits & Vegetables
Bacon	Meat Products
Bacon Bits	Sugar, Spices & Sweeteners
Bandages	Medical
Barbeque Sauce	Condiments
Batteries	Electronics
Bean Dip	Salsa, Spreads & Dips
Beans	Canned Beans & Chili
Bottled Water	Water
Bouillon	Soup
Chicken	Meat Products
Chili	Canned Beans & Chili
Cocoa	Chocolate
Cold Remedies	Medical
Condensed Milk	Baked Goods & Baking Supplies
Cooking Oil & Spray	Oil & Vinegar
Corn Meal	Baked Goods & Baking Supplies

Lip Balm	Body Care
Margarine	Butter & Margarine
Marshmallows	Baked Goods & Baking Supplies
Mayonnaise	Condiments
Molasses	Sugar, Spices & Sweeteners
Mouthwash	Dental Care
MSG	Sugar, Spices & Sweeteners
Mustard	Condiments
Noodles	Soups & Noodles
Nuts	Popcorn, Nuts & Pretzels
Office/Copy Paper	Paper
Package Delivery	Office Supplies
Pain Relievers	Medical
Pancake Mix	Breakfast Food
Pencils & Pens	Office Supplies
Pickles	Olives & Pickles
Pies	Desserts
Potato Chips	Chips
Pretzels	Popcorn, Nuts & Pretzels
Pudding	Dairy Products
Relishes	Olives & Pickles
Rice Milk	Milk & Alternatives
Salt	Sugar, Spices & Sweeteners
School Supplies	Office Supplies
Shampoo	Hair Care

Shaving Needs	Body Care
Sherbet	Ice Cream & Alternatives
Shortening	Oil & Vinegar
Soft Drinks	Soda
Soy Milk	Milk & Alternatives
Sports Drinks	Energy Drinks
Stuffing Mix	Bread & Bread Crumbs
Sun Block	Body Care
Syrup	Sugar, Spices & Sweeteners
Tahini	Peanut Butter & Jelly
Tampons	Feminine Care
Tape	Office Supplies
Tissues	Paper Towels & Toilet Paper
Tofu	Meat Alternatives
Toilet Paper	Paper Towels & Toilet Paper
Tomato Paste	Pasta & Sauce
Toothbrushes	Dental Care
Toothpaste	Dental Care
Tortilla Chips	Chips
Tuna	Seafood
Veggie Burgers	Meat Alternatives
Vinegar	Oil & Vinegar
Waffles	Breakfast Food
Whipped Cream	Dairy Products
Yogurt	Dairy Products

DO YOUR OWN RESEARCH

Berne Declaration
   www.evb.ch/en
Better Business Bureau
   www.bbb.org/bizethics
Business Ethics
   www.business-ethics.com
Business for Social Responsibility
   www.bsr.org
Center For Public Integrity
   www.publicintegrity.org
CERES Principles
   www.ceres.org
Clean Clothes Campaign
   www.cleanclothes.org
Clean Computer Campaign
   www.svtc.org/cleancc
Co-op America
   www.coopamerica.org
Corporate Accountability
   www.stopcorporateabuse.org
Corporate Knights
   www.corporateknights.ca
Corpwatch
   www.corpwatch.org
Covalence Ethical Quotations
   www.covalence.ch

Ethical Consumer
    www.ethicalconsumer.org
FTSE4Good Index
    www.ftse.com
Global Sullivan Principles
    www.thegsp.org
Hoover's
    www.hoovers.com
Human Rights Campaign
    www.hrc.org
Multinational Monitor
    www.multinationalmonitor.org
People for the Ethical Treatment of Animals
    www.peta.org
Responsible Shopper
    www.responsibleshopper.org
Social Venture Network
    www.svn.org
Transfair USA
    www.transfairusa.org
Union of Concerned Scientists
    www.ucsusa.org
U.S. Environmental Protection Agency
    www.epa.gov
World Environment Center
    www.wec.org

About the author

Since receiving his doctoral degree from University of Colorado, Boulder, **Ellis Jones** has focused all of his energies on bridging the gap between academics, activists and the average citizen. A scholar of social responsibility, global citizenship and everyday activism, Ellis continues to teach and give presentations on how to turn lofty ideals into practical actions around the country. Following three years as Assistant Professor of Sociology and Director of Service Learning at Sacramento City College, Ellis now teaches sociology at University of California, Davis. He is the founder of The Better World Network and co-author of *The Better World Handbook*.

If you have enjoyed *The Better World Shopping Guide*
you might also enjoy other

BOOKS TO BUILD A NEW SOCIETY

Our books provide positive solutions for people who want to
make a difference. We specialize in:

Environment and Justice • Conscientious Commerce
Sustainable Living • Ecological Design and Planning
Natural Building & Appropriate Technology • Nonviolence
Educational and Parenting Resources • Progressive Leadership

New Society Publishers
ENVIRONMENTAL BENEFITS STATEMENT

New Society Publishers has chosen to produce this book on Enviro
100, recycled paper made with **100% post consumer waste**,
processed chlorine free, and old growth free.

For every 5,000 books printed, New Society saves the following
resources:[1]

9	Trees
788	Pounds of Solid Waste
867	Gallons of Water
1,130	Kilowatt Hours of Electricity
1,432	Pounds of Greenhouse Gases
6	Pounds of HAPs, VOCs, and AOX Combined
2	Cubic Yards of Landfill Space

[1]Environmental benefits are calculated based on research done by the
Environmental Defense Fund and other members of the Paper Task Force who
study the environmental impacts of the paper industry.

For a full list of NSP's titles, please call **1-800-567-6772**
or check out our website at: **www.newsociety.com**

NEW SOCIETY PUBLISHERS